Why I Am for the Church

WHY I AM FOR THE CHURCH

TALKS ON RELIGION AND POLITICS

By Charles P. Taft

FARRAR, STRAUS AND COMPANY
NEW YORK, 1947

PRINTED IN THE UNITED STATES OF AMERICA
BY THE MAPLE PRESS COMPANY, YORK, PA.

Preface

Many years ago, after a particularly bad speech before a critical group of oldsters in Cincinnati, then my new home, I bewailed the failure to my father. He wrote me not to worry, that speaking was largely practice, and that I should accept every invitation to speak that anyone would give me. He was right. Practice gave confidence and facility.

But speaking gave something else. It required thought and research and it reflected current reading and current activity. Over a period of time a man's speeches begin to reflect the development of a philosophy.

So it is that these addresses have something of a sameness and yet embroider the design with some developing variations. I have tried to eliminate the repetitions, except in a few important matters. The statism and the envious materialism of Marx on the one hand, and the Christian love for God and neighbor and emphasis on personality as the basis for modern democracy on the other, are so vital in our modern political and religious struggle that one can hardly avoid some restatement.

CHARLES P. TAFT

January 30, 1947

Contents

CHAPTER ONE

A Theory of Living [1]

*W*ITH THE INFINITE SUBDIVISION OF MATTER and the infinite expansion of the universe, principles that have guided our ancestors have been profoundly modified or have disappeared altogether. What we took to be foundation stones of economics, politics and religion are shaking, and their very existence is open to serious question. With so many people brought so close together in such complicated relationships, it becomes intensely difficult to work out any satisfactory synthesis. We are deafened by the conflicting shouts of specialists, and few indeed are the voices that are simple, lovely, strong and altogether satisfying.

TECHNOLOGY AND A JOB

These preliminary remarks may impress you as rather abstract, and your first question is apt to be: How can I get a job? Are six million to continue unemployed even with the return of prosperity? Are the technocrats right when they say today's college graduates may never find work?

I cannot tell you what job to look for or where to find it. No one but yourself can tell you what you should do with your life. But I can tell you that there are very definite trends in vocations and that it will help you to pick the brains of those who are expert students of those trends. You may be interested in a few sample generalizations. Thanks to technology, a lessening portion of the world's work is being done by sweat and muscle, by a strong back and a weak mind. Teachers have increased tenfold since 1870; even more rapid has been the increase in technical engineers, nurses,

[1] Talk before graduating class of Randolph-Macon College, Ashland, Virginia, June 12, 1934. Printed in *Vital Speeches of The Day*, 1937.

draftsmen, musicians, artists, actors, chemists, librarians, and authors. Some of those classifications have been seriously affected in recent years, either temporarily or permanently. But in general it can be said that opportunities lie in increasing numbers in occupations in which effectiveness in personal relations is indispensable, such as managing, selling, nursing, instructing, and social work. There is less hardship in those fields than among mechanics and craftsmen. The bulk of unemployment has been in the durable goods industries rather than in those whose contact is directly with the public. If it is true that we have solved the problem of how to produce the goods we all need, then with improved distribution will come a continuing increase in chances to work with people, serving their wants, supervising their joint efforts, getting their hearty co-operation, managing them, persuading them, teaching them, helping them.

WHERE THE COLLEGE FAILS

Your educational process has given you little enough basis for these activities to be sure. There are occasionally good courses in effective public speaking, in clear, colorful exposition of ideas, or in personnel management. I have yet to find anywhere lessons in that art which most people require at one time or another—training in human understanding, emotional control, sincerity, tact, courtesy, poise, and diction. The fact that we have no textbooks on those subjects is no reason for passing them up. After all the oil companies have been able to train oil-station attendants. Such a course combined with one in public relations should be required for graduation from every college and university.

Are you worried about technocracy? Let me take you back to 1790 in our United States. In order to produce the textiles used in 1930 upon the equipment available in 1790, it would take fifteen billion people working ten hours a day. If modern methods of wheat cultivation had been suggested 140 years ago, our ancestors would have been horrified at the number to be thrown out of work. But using their methods all the farmers who produce any kind of crop would have to work on wheat alone to produce our normal crop today. Has textile machinery thrown fifteen billions out of work, or agricultural machinery forty millions? We cannot foresee the direction or character of normal industrial expansion, but we can acquire a better sense of proportion if we realize how little our ancestors of a hundred years ago, who lived in the midst of just as great confusion, unemployment and dislocation as we do, could see their way out. So I say to you, study occupational trends and your own capacities and place yourself where your life will count most effectively for human service.

YOU NEED A THEORY OF LIVING

Serious as your problem may be to find a job, it is far more important to you and those whose lives you influence whether you approach both your job and your life outside your job with a theory of living. I don't mean that you are prepared now, or should be, to set forth in stately words a philosophy of life; but you ought to be thinking about its meaning so far as you can see it and state to yourself for your own satisfaction what principles you value as guides. You can't see the end. Oliver Cromwell once said, "No man goes so far as he who cannot see whither he goes." But you can build up, as he did, your guiding principles slowly and purposefully.

I suggest to you first that you develop a philosophy of history, an idea of progress. The ancient Greeks thought of history as a progressive and inevitable degeneration and decay. Some of them believed in world cycles beginning with a golden age, and repeating in the minutest particular the events of each previous cycle, a monotonous iteration unlikely to stimulate interest in the future. In the Middle Ages, the Christian theory worked out by St. Augustine assumed that the whole movement of human history was for the purpose of securing the happiness of a few in another world. Providence intervened constantly to bring that about, and once the predetermined number were provided for, the world might just as well end. No longer was there any cyclical movement, but a steady historical trend toward the ultimate City of God, not on earth which was evil, but in heaven.

THE IDEA OF CONDORCET

Not until the time of Condorcet, during the French Revolution, and Saint Simon, Comte, and Spencer less than a hundred years ago, did the idea of progress, of the evolution of human society in a mighty movement toward perfection, really begin to seize upon the imagination of men. There are a few today who scoff, but I commend to you nevertheless, as a start for your theory of living, the idea of Condorcet that human progress is a conscious and active movement toward the ideal commonwealth, and that each generation has in considerable measure the power to determine the forms and workings of its own institutions.

This involves a number of other ideas. The first and most important is that, since you are dealing with human nature, progress toward the ideal in respect of any matters deep in the human soul, must be a gradual process of evolution. If things move too fast there is likely to be a recession to compensate. The state cannot create the ideal commonwealth by fiat of law, as can be seen in such homely examples as the experience with prohibition, as well as in efforts to regulate handbooks (racehorse betting at the neighborhood magazine stand or drugstore). But the state can guide an educational process designed to bring home to the individual his responsibility as a citizen, and it can raise the minimum standards of health, safety, and social welfare when the educational process has created sufficient public sentiment to back it in maintaining those standards. For the establishment of the higher standards toward which we aim, there is nothing upon which we can rely except the slow process of education of individuals. You may think that idea too slow for the uprising youth of today, but as you read history with the seeing eye you find that permanent progress has come that way.

HISTORY AS A GUIDE

One trouble with most of us when we come to establish our philosophy of life as applied to politics is that we give ourselves so little background. If history is an evolutionary process we must understand some of the past in order to see any light in the present.

I suppose I studied Hegel at college, and I know that my boss in the Army gave me Hegel's *Philosophy of History* some time ago. Hegel glorified the state and regarded its authority as inevitably embodied in an autocratic and powerful government. He recognized a sovereignty of the general will but restricted knowledge of that general will to wise rulers. He believed that a moral and rational exaltation of the state elevates the citizens spiritually. He must have talked about 100 per cent Prussianism. His followers believe that the state, for all citizens and in all matters, is the highest arbiter of conduct and opinion and is entitled to choose its own means, violent or otherwise, of vindicating its supremacy.

This idea of the totalitarian state found its highest expression in the last century in Russia, and it is no longer surprising, if you note my suggestion about the evolution of history, to find the same absolutism and the same swallowing up of the individual in the interests of the state in the Soviet Republic. The fascist philosophers, Croce and Gentile, have given the most recent expression in philosophy of this idea, and Hitler is its latest exponent in fact.

I tell you of Hegel because it is Hegel and his descendants whom we are battling, you and I who believe in democracy. Against the theory of Hegel we find France, England, and the United States standing together in the same democratic tradition as do no others of the nations of the world. We may be disappointed when German or Italian democracy fails. But we three, we cannot fail or the tradition dies. Democracy has its faults clearly enough but, as Bryce said, "However grave the indictment that may be brought against democracy, its friends can answer 'What better alternative can you offer?' " Democracy in the best sense calls into activity the intelligence and character of the ordinary man and woman. Our forefathers have died for that ideal and for the destruction of absolutism. The view that only the ruler knows the general will and that any means, however cruel, violent or oppressive, are justified for the establishment of the state—"My country, right or wrong!—" can never appeal to the liberal, the man who stands for freedom. So I give you as another article of your philosophy of living a belief in democracy and the common sense of ordinary people in the long run.

AN HONEST DEMOCRACY

Your theories need in these days a more specific application to the problem of government. In every city and town and county today is stirring an interest in local government which after all is the heart of democratic living. So I suggest to you a few principles that have been worked out in these last forty years of struggle for honest local administration in the interest of the people.,

The frame of government should be simple and easily understood.

The questions of policy should be decided by a small legislative body elected at large, preferably by proportional representation.

The administrative function should be handled by an experienced administrator, and, as the qualities that produce votes for oneself are not usually associated with administrative ability, the legislative body should pick the administrator. Other forms work sometimes when operated by good men, but given men of the same ability the small council-manager form works best. Especially is it adapted to amateur political organization for the establishment and maintenance of good government.

Above all don't let anyone ever convince you that there is any consideration that should influence your vote and action except the welfare of the citizens of today and their descendants. In some communities the welfare of the national parties, in others the traditions of long accepted custom, are invoked against movements for good government.

When Jeremy Bentham a hundred years ago attacked the outrageous and unbelievable abuses of the English law courts, he was told by Edmund Burke that when ancient opinions and rules of life are taken away we have no compass to govern us, nor can we know distinctly to what port we steer. In modern times such excellent tools of democracy as proportional representation, of which even we Irish approve, are called un-American. Loyalty to a party machine is exalted above economical service to the people of the community because forsooth without the local spoils system the national party could not operate successfully. At least so we are told, although it must be fairly clear that men guilty of corruption in national affairs received their training in spoils locally. English parties have operated now these many years without local patronage. The good of the city and its people is the first and only consideration in local government. Nail that to your masthead.

THE MARX PROGRAM OF ACTION

You must face, whatever your occupation, the problems of industrial and economic organization, and fit them into your philosophy of life. Here, too, you must go back into history, and I suggest that you begin with Karl Marx. Wickham Steed, the Liberal, English journalist, advises the reading of the "Communist Manifesto" at least once a year. Though written in 1848 you will find it strikingly modern, and many of its phrases are familiar because we hear them frequently upon the lips of socialist and labor leaders today.

Marx taught that economic stress operating through the relations of production (landlord to tenant, lord to vassal, factory-owner to wage-laborer) determined the whole cultural order and its institutions in any period in history. He denied that spiritual influences such as ideals of justice, freedom, or religion were anything but cloaks for the realities of economic strife.

He argued that since labor produces all wealth, laborers had the right to the whole produce of labor. And because they did not get the surplus value of the produce above the wages paid them, there was and always had been a difference in economic status between labor and the owners of the means of production. History, said Marx, is a series of struggles by the exploited against the exploiters, class against class; this struggle is inevitable and it may be bloody; only through it can the classless society be achieved.

There is much of Marx that is uncomfortably true. You can find the same materialist interpretation of history in Charles A. Beard's writings. You can find any number of Christian ministers who give emphasis to the class struggle by their bitter descriptions of the contrast between the excesses of the idle rich and the misery of the downtrodden poor. And your own observations give point to much of what Marx expresses so pungently. Much of his analysis of history cannot be denied.

As to a program of action, Marx is somewhat ambiguous, with the result that his followers have divided rather sharply between those who reject any step but revolution and the dictatorship of the proletariat, and the revisionists who are willing to use ordinary political methods to secure power and will accept partial reforms, such as minimum wage laws and child labor laws, as half loaves and better than none.

What are you and I to think of Marx? Shall we say "Red" with a shudder and close our eyes to all but a vision of a bogey man in a bushy beard labeled "Bolshie"? Or shall we analyze just why we don't like Marx and say so? I recommend the scientific method.

I don't like Marx, first, because I believe (with some great socialist leaders) that historical changes have been prepared and carried through mainly by spiritual influences such as the idea of justice and freedom, which inspired men to struggle for their ideals. Will you base your life on the theory that every man has his price, or, to put it more politely, that however great men may be, they lead the people for reasons that grow out of their economic status in the community; or will you set up ideals to steer your ship by and stick with them in storm and stress? That is no rhetorical question, for Beard and Marx can quote chapter and verse in the lives of great men who have by their practice sustained the materialist interpretation of history. Yet I still say you cannot drive God out of history or men's lives.

I dislike Marx and his followers because they insist upon the inevitability of class struggle. His followers today will on occasion do their utmost to prevent the settlement on a fair basis of industrial disputes. They insist on struggle and refuse the method found essential in every human relationship of trial and error, compromise and evolution.

Marx has proved wrong in the idea that the worker must grow steadily poorer, at least as far as the large industrial countries are concerned. It is also untrue that wealth has concentrated in fewer and fewer hands, for there has been a gradual spreading of the ownership of wealth. It is true in this country, however, that half the corporate wealth of the country is concentrated in two hundred corporations out of more than twenty thousand. The development of the modern corporation, which has crept up on us almost without our knowing it, is the most significant thing in industry today. For as Adolph Berle has shown, the millions of stockholders of those corporations have little or nothing to say about the management. Only 11 per cent of the companies with 6 per cent of the assets are run by the majority stockholders. Sixty-five per cent of the companies with 80 per cent of the assets are run by the management or by small stockholders through a legal device.

Does this situation cause the kind of exploitation of the workers predicted by Marx? In some cases it has. Companies import cheap labor from backward districts and, when they learn the going rate and demand it, throw them on the streets. In others the attitude toward labor has been progressive and fair.

It depends on the moral and ethical standards of the management. The standards of ethics in city government have been low. Many think they reflected the prevailing ethics in business. The standards of city government are rising, and it seems fair to assume the standards of business are also rising. In both cases the improvement comes, be it noted, not by law, but by the stirring of individual consciences.

ELEMENTS IN CORPORATE CONTROL

In these two hundred great corporations there are four main elements to be considered. I name them in the traditional order of their importance: the shareholders, the management, the wage-earners, and the consumers or the public. By importance I mean their relative power to insist upon a share in the profits of the business.

In one typical situation the management are no longer shareholders to any substantial degree, and the shareholders are so numerous as to be unorganized and without a voice. The traditional order then is changed and the management comes ahead of the shareholders, at least until publicity at the annual meeting or through the Federal Trade Commission curbs their power.

When the corporation is a public utility governed by a state commission, the consumer who is otherwise last may move rapidly to the first place, so that the order of importance would be consumer, management, stockholders and wage-earners. It is conceivable that by a threat of a strike at a psychological moment, that is, by the method of class war, the wage-earners might for that moment reach an equality at the top with the consuming public.

What is the proper order of these interests? I suggest to you that the first lien upon the gross earnings of any company is a living wage for its employees. If the business is such that it cannot pay a living wage, then the sooner it quits the better. The most difficult cases under the NRA are restaurants and hand laundries. The marginal companies pay even in big cities from $3 to $6 per week. I have no hesitation in saying that if they cannot pay more they should be driven out of business.

MANAGEMENT AS TRUSTEE

The management is or should be in the position of a trustee for the three other interests. It should be compensated in accordance with its ability, but any man who thinks he is worth a million a year has a bad case of expanded ego. I have no sympathy with the current demagoguery that would limit any salary to $8,500 a year or less, but there is to my mind a very definite limitation upon the amount a trustee should pay himself for his services.

The consumer is represented badly or well in the management of public service corporations by the state public utility commissions.

As yet his only connection with the management of other corporations is when he is on the receiving end of its advertising. I wonder what will be the first corporation to provide for direct consumer representation in its management? And how soon will management recognize the right of the consumer to share in increased profit? It is the pressure of competition, on the idea of larger profits by larger production at lower prices, that has given this share up to date.

The stockholder's return is definitely limited in certain industries affected with a public interest. Theoretically it is unlimited in all other cases. But in fact the increase of profits produces sharing with management first, then usually with workmen and perhaps even with consumers by reduction in prices. Is the lack of limitation on profits socially sound? There is a respectable fund of experience in England, the United States, and the Antipodes, that would demonstrate the possibility of limiting profits to shareholders and giving the workmen a stake in the concern as partners in some form. An unlimited return is not necessary to get capital even for risky undertakings, though of course the risk must be paid for.

The idea of a real and legal partnership between workers and the other elements in the company is, it seems to me, the only alternative to the bitterness of class struggle in our industrial order. Don't permit anyone to tell you it is impossible. It is being done. The extremists may say it is a camouflage for more exploitation. But I tell you it is the only solution which is Christian. It is not the greatly overrated profit motive which causes our trouble in business today. It is the absence of the willingness to give up our absolutism, our sovereignty of each individual and each company in favor of a true and legal democracy of the kind to which we all give lip service in politics. For partnership is democracy and is the only way to social peace in industry.

A CHRISTIAN PHILOSOPHY

And the final test of your philosophy, gentlemen, to my mind is whether it is Christian—that is, like Christ's. Christ showed us what God was, a loving father, and he showed us the infinite capacity of the human soul to approach the divine ideal. I have spoken of the idea of progress, of perfectibility. That surely is Christian, and it must look to the day when peace comes to a world torn with strife. The patience required for the slow evolution of society by the winning of individuals through persuasion is characteristic of the way Christ won the world. No one who established as He did the dignity of human personality and re-emphasized the foundations of ethics, could yield for a moment to the state in terms of Hegel, Lenin, Gentile and Hitler, with its complete absence of ethical basis. Loving your neighbor as yourself is irreconcilable with the class struggle.

I do not mean to say that you can find a guide in the Bible or in religion to every step you are called upon to take in the life that commences today. But I do say that you will work out, consciously or unconsciously, a theory of living that will cover most of the field I have touched upon. I suggest that it will be a better theory if you do it consciously. And I am sure that if you steep your mind and soul in the lives and thoughts of the great figures of the Bible, whose record is worn smooth with the touch of millions of lives, you will find a greater satisfaction and perform a greater service for your day and generation in those fields which in these days no man can avoid, politics and industry.

CHAPTER TWO

Why I Am for the Church[1]

A VERY WISE AND EXPERIENCED PUBLIC speaker once said that a speech could never catch the attention of an audience unless it answered a question for which the audience wanted an answer. I am sure many people are asking themselves in the silent hours, *Should I be for the church?*

That question is part of a larger problem that faces all of us much of the time. We are all engaged in a more or less intense effort to find some thread upon which to string the essential facts of human experience as a guide through a world that often impresses one as slightly insane.

Arnold Toynbee has been engaged in writing a history of the twenty-one different civilizations that have existed in man's experience. In the first of these volumes he calls attention to what he describes as the rhythm of history. In the eighteenth century, for instance, men were primarily interested in organizing accumulated material. That was the age of Gibbon, of the encyclopaedists, of a critic like Voltaire. In the nineteenth century, says Mr. Toynbee, man was enlarging the sources of knowledge and creating a vast bulk of information, without much effort at analysis.

While the process is still continuing in some degree, most men, with a feeling of utter confusion, are seeking simplification, and for one reason or another some men are trying to satisfy their need. Wells began it with *The Outline of History*. We have had many outlines of science. Toynbee's massive work is of the same character. Harry Elmer Barnes and Will Durant have entered the same field.

[1] Printed in the *Christian Century Pulpit*, February 1937.

13

GOD IN HUMAN HISTORY

In all this confusion, I am for the church in the first place because it insists upon the presence of God in human history. As I read the history of the church, this was not always the case. Certainly the primitive churches, which looked for the immediate return of Christ bringing with him the judgment day, had little interest in politics and business of their day. Paul was hard put to it to explain to the early Christians how some of their friends and dear ones were allowed to die before the second coming. They had no hope for an improvement on earth, and in many cases their fears had considerable basis.

A philosophy of history which took account of any prospective improvement, or sought to find any past record of improvement in human living, was first set out in reasoned form by the great German, Hegel. During his time began what is called the idea of progress. That this idea should be so new always startles me a little, because most of us take the "bigger and better" ideals of the Chamber of Commerce and the Booster Club as something that has always existed.

Hegel found a record of gradual improvement in human history in spite of its ups and downs. But curiously enough, when Karl Marx, his most famous student, analyzed the course of history, he went to the opposite extreme and saw no consistent thread except the contrasting methods of earning a living. Religion, idealism, and all spiritual motives he discounted almost completely. At least he held that these were mere shams used by the dominant classes of society to keep down the proletariat.

This theory of Marx and Engels produced its natural reaction, and Thomas H. Green laid the basis for the idealistic view of history. He has been followed by such historians and philosophers as H. A. L. Fisher, of England, and Benedetto Croce, of Italy. In the socialist movement itself came some reaction, and no finer expression of the idealistic viewpoint has been given than by Jaures, the great Frenchman who died just before the war.

So I say that I am for the church because it insists upon the presence of God in human history. It insists that man's relationship to God is his religion, and it refuses to be satisfied with the humanism that makes mere service a substitute "just as good."

I do not mean that the church has always made clear its position, but certainly it cannot avoid this position, no other organization can assert it so strongly, and no other ideal can more inspire the church. It brings with it a discontent with conditions in which we live, which is surely divine, and a sense of need in every human soul.

THE CHURCH AND HUMAN PERSONALITY

I am for the church also because it insists upon the importance of human personality, and asserts the divine capacity of every individual no matter how degraded.

It is of considerable interest to me that the beginnings of democracy grew directly from the religious insistence upon individual conscience. In the sixteenth and seventeenth centuries, the dissenting groups in England—beginning with the Anabaptists and following with the Quakers and the dissenting Puritans, who broke away from the Anglican church—developed the small independent congregation which governed itself. In these small groups of men and women convinced that God spoke to each of them, people were ready to listen to each other with tolerance until everyone had spoken, and then decide in accordance with the will of the majority. As Cromwell put it, the will of the majority was likely to be the true will of God for such a congregation.

During this same period came the growth of science, beginning with Newton, and this left an impression on men's minds of a mechanistic world, in which a human being was an atom of no importance, crushed in the machine. This, too, led to the idea that the king was no better than the commoner. When John Locke tried to explain the "glorious revolution" of 1688 and told the world that government existed only by the consent of the governed, he was drawing together these two threads to form the beginning of the philosophy of democracy.

Hegel is responsible too, for a development which in its essentials is opposed not only to democracy but to religion in this very matter which I am discussing. While he agreed that the will of the people should prevail, he said that only the few, and perhaps only the divinely appointed ruler, *Der Führer*, could really know what that will was; and that the character of the individual must be refined by his submission to whatever the ruling group felt were the necessities of the state. This totalitarian idea now operating in Russia, Germany and Italy is fundamentally opposed not only to democracy, but essentially to the Christian ideal for human personality. Russia could permit millions to starve because the good of the state was felt to demand it. No Christian can believe that. Because this conflict is one of the few great conflicts of the day, I am for the church, which must stand four-square on the teachings of Christ. I am for one of his most distinctive teachings, namely, that God is interested in every human soul.

THE WORLD AND HUMAN PERSONALITY

I am for the church in the third place because it is the company of faithful people. In saying this I am not expressing an attitude of "holier than thou." I am simply testifying to the general characteristics of people whom I meet in church. Besides that, I am constantly finding that people whom I meet and work with in other enterprises, and in whom I find I can put the greatest confidence, are sincere members of some religious group.

I hope it will be quite clear that I am not considering the church in any exclusive sense, but rather in the same sense as Christ's famous parable in which he attempted to describe his neighbor.

This third reason needs only one additional comment, that it surely applies to church members in neighboring counties, neighboring states and neighboring nations, in a day when the most distant corners of the earth have been brought in fact next to us.

Lastly, I am for the church because it seems to me that there is greater need of God, and of human personalities with divine ideals, at the present time and in the days that are coming, than ever before. Confused as people in many ages have been, there has never been a day when there was a greater undigested mass of facts and circumstances pressing in upon us, nor a day with problems more difficult to solve. If we think of social relationships, of money, exchange, unemployment and other economic problems, of the struggle to find adequate principles of political science to guide us in the "endless adventure of governing men," as Oliver called it, surely we must agree that men of idealism and of religious strength can contribute more than any other group to the advance of mankind.

No field needs religion more than the international. There is no possible answer to violent, destructive nationalism except principles worked out upon the basis of love of God and one's neighbor, and I know of no way in which nationalism in other countries can be opposed and overcome except through the support of foreign missions. Not only because the world is one today but because we of the Occident are primarily responsible for the spread of industrialism to Japan, China, and India, we must help to build up a nucleus of native church people and through them a public opinion in those nations which can help to bring at the very least the advances in factory and child labor legislation which we have achieved. I am not proposing a destruction of the other great religions, but their inspiration to join and help the Christian church in fighting secularism, nationalism, and abuses of industrialism.

Neither am I advocating a social gospel which in some cases may be properly described as somewhat fanatic and often badly educated in history and economics. I oppose with equal fervor a static conservatism in the church, which is hostile to change, invariably defends the established order, and usually protects privilege.

PESSIMIST AND OPTIMIST

It seems to me that the struggle in which we all are involved is well summed up in the contrast between the royal pessimist who wrote the Book of Ecclesiastes, and the thoughtful optimist named Paul.

Said the pessimist:

I hated all that I had toiled at under the sun, knowing that I must leave it to the man who follows me, and who knows whether he will be a wise man or a fool?

So I saw the best thing for man was to be happy in his work; that is what he gets out of life, for who can show him what is to happen afterwards?

Naked he came from his mother's womb and naked he must return; for all his toil he has nothing to take with him.

Anyone still alive has something to live for (even a live dog is better than a dead lion); the living know this at least, that they must die.

Sow your seed in the morning of life and stay not your hand till evening; you never know whether this or that shall prosper or whether both shall have success.

Said the optimist:

We triumph even in our troubles, knowing that trouble produces endurance, endurance produces character, and character produces hope—a hope which never disappoints us, since God's love floods our hearts through the Holy Spirit which has been given to us.

CHAPTER THREE

Wise Men or Fools[1]

WE ARE AS A NATION GROWING OLDER; A larger proportion of people each year is over sixty-five and a smaller proportion is under twenty-five. Each year we have to fight harder to overcome the discouragment of age, and to cultivate the very life blood of our nation—the energy, imagination, and initiative of young men and women. I need hardly remind you that young men won the American Revolution, wrote the Constitution, and made the new government work.

But why should the youth of today be the center of our attention? Why do we watch the young men and women of the new generation with curiosity and irritation and anger and affection? Because each of us knows that we must leave our work unto the man that shall come after us, and who knows whether he shall be a wise man or a fool?

THE REVOLUTIONARY PAST

We do well to cultivate the past if we do it with discrimination and common sense. You and I and especially the youth of today need a sense of the continuity of history. History probably does not repeat itself, but it is a procession, not a series of disconnected tableaux. Moreover it is like a procession of elephants with the tail of one in the trunk of the next. Let me break into the procession for a moment at the point of the American Revolution.

The American Revolution was a social movement, as Dr.

[1] Address before the Continental Congress of the Daughters of the American Revolution, April 22, 1937, Washington, D.C. Printed in *Social Progress*, June, 1937.

Jameson showed more than ten years ago, and its leaders were vigorous young men who were not afraid of being called subversive influences. I can't help thinking that Governor Hutchinson, whose history of the Massachusetts Bay Colony has just been reprinted, must have felt toward Samuel Adams and John Hancock a good deal as some high automobile officials feel toward sit-down strikers. The wild Irish immigrants, among whom I number some of my ancestors, did a lot of the fighting for us in 1776, while a lot of the "best people" were British sympathizers, who after the Peace Treaty were driven out of the Colonies to Canada. As they trudged sorrowfully northward into the wilderness of Ontario, as they looked back in the next four years upon the quarrels, jealousies, weakness, and confusion of the United States under the Confederation, they must have felt that much of their own lives had been wasted, and wished like Richard II to sit upon the ground and tell sad stories of the death of progress if not of kings.

But they were wrong, and it was youth joining hands with experience that picked up the torch from the past and moulded that matchless instrument of government, the Constitution of the United States. The constitution did not spring full panoplied from the brow of Jove; it grew from the distilled wisdom of the greatest political thinkers of the last two thousand years, adapted to the needs of our own country by those keen minds of the Convention who gave honor to the title politician. The document which those men shaped and smoothed will live through crises even greater than the one through which it has just passed, because those men put in it the qualities of youth and life.

But the Revolution did not end with the Treaty of Peace or the Constitution. Do you remember that in the states only one person in twenty-five could vote in 1789? My state of Ohio put manhood suffrage in its constitution in 1803, but it took the Dorr rebellion in 1841 to do it in Rhode Island and not until 1850 did the last state go along. They called that the Jeffersonian and the Jacksonian Revolution, but Jefferson and Jackson were only the symbols. It was a revolution of youth, of young frontier families, and the Methodist and Baptist revival had a lot to do with it.

A LOOK AT MODERN TIMES

Look at modern times with that revolutionary past marshaled behind them, and surely you will understand youth better. Millions of men and women today do need work, and often when they get a job, it is in an organization whose constitution and frame of government is closer to the authoritarian state than to the democratic self-government of a free people. Young people are excited about that. Perhaps they do emphasize too much the dark side of modern times, but it does the rest of us no good to close our eyes to it. How can we marshal the energy of youth, and join hands to make a better world?

We must begin by intelligent observation of the younger generation. In many parts of the world they have come together in mass movements, marshaled behind programs that promise to cure the ills of the world. England and the United States have not seen that phenomenon in its full force; perhaps we may never see it. But the influence of the ideas in those mass movements we cannot escape. Young people are disturbed and finally aroused by economic insecurity, the denial of a chance to make their contribution to progress. They are tremendously stirred by the ideal of peace in our time. They have a real passion, many of them, for the underdog. They are offered the sure cure of the medicine men, and over against it they see only a well-meaning philanthropy, bumbling self-seeking politicians, and reactionary manufacturers. At least so they are told and so they believe. In a modern scientific world they are sometimes as sentimental as lavender and old lace, and occasionally like their elders they swallow as gospel propositions lacking any semblance of logic and reason.

But how can you meet that situation? You can't do it by trying to compete with the promisers. The most unscrupulous and ruthless will always win out in that kind of competition. The panaceas of the social gospel and production for use, for instance, and all the other tag-words of the intellectuals, become a little silly when the brickbat crashes through the factory windows, or the man on horseback appears on the avenue.

Neither can you get anywhere by preaching liberty, damning fascist dictators, or painting red networks of communism across every evening sky. I don't say that because those sermons and curses are false, although many are. I say it because nobody is converted by that process of controversy. The one who shouts about communism is always discounted as a fascist at heart. The Liberty League becomes the whipping boy of the have-nots.

Especially futile are the current efforts to identify pacifism with socialism. Young people hate war with a deep hatred, and they should. They will never admit that it is inevitable. They demand that it be stamped out like disease. They cannot see why "defense" means protection of foreign trade and foreign investments, and they ask with some reason, I must say—why we should spend a billion and a quarter dollars a year for that defense without any reliable study of what we are defending and how we should do the job. That may be wrong, but it is the product of intelligent cerebration and should be treated as such.

RECIPE FOR THE TREATMENT OF YOUTH

Well, what can you do with these irritating young whippersnappers, then—like me? With some trepidation I offer a recipe for the treatment of youth in modern times.

Begin with a big self-application of patience. I don't mean something lazy and passive. I mean the kind of endurance that produces character and hope. That kind of patience grows from convictions of your own, that are tough and elastic from rubbing against other contrary convictions; they are not something hard and brittle from a protected life. Don't forget that steel is the most elastic substance we know—it gives and springs back into place. And it is designed even to resist destructive stresses and strains, without censorship. We are going through hard times for those that love and appreciate tradition. But remember that traditions were once innovations; remember that we had to have the five terrible years of the Confederation in order to get the Constitution;

and remember that the Constitution itself was close to revolutionary in its day.

Give youth responsibility and experience. How can young people learn otherwise? We shut them out from participation in life itself and then damn them for trying to set up an artificial life of their own. I don't believe in youth movements because I want youth in the stream of life, but I am not surprised at what they do when they can't get into the stream. It is just like damning labor unions for being irresponsible in bargaining when they are given responsibility only for war, not for bargaining. War breeds ruthlessness, peace breeds honor. For labor unions and for youth, give them a chance and give them time.

Build a real love of country that endures 365 days in the year. Its foundation must be a love of land and soil and neighborhood, difficult as that is for an urban and a mobile people. Perhaps it is the feel of the soil about the plow, or the loveliness of the parks and little garden plots and flowering trees bursting into color. Or it may be the familiar vista and the old rock with the carved initials, or the familiar corner of the old haunts with the worn table and the voices of old friends. Doesn't that feeling for country make you rage down deep in your soul when you see some of the eyesores vile men make or the wrecks of human lives that equally vile men help to produce? I rode through the near South recently and saw farm after farm whose once black soil, was bare red gullies. Like trees, only God can make top soil and I wanted to cheer when I passed one lonely farm whose tenant was trying to help Him by brushfilling the gullies and contour plowing and ditching. Youth understands city and country planning for land and water and mineral resources, for streets and housing and public buildings. That, I say, is part of patriotism to young men and women today.

THE CHIEF INGREDIENT IS LOVE

To youth love of country is all inextricably mixed with love of people, individual people. The real heart of our democracy began with the conviction of the Levelers in England three hundred years ago that the poorest he in England had a life to live as the richest he. There is no sight like that of a great minister of God in a downtown church, welding into a huge but very real family people from every walk of life, and building in each one a feeling that he or she is making some contribution to the community life. Young people fit into that family and young people get excited when members of that family suffer. They demand, and rightly, that every one of us shall be concerned with that suffering and do something about it. They want action and they are entitled to get it.

But young people today are bred with the scientific spirit. They may be taken in for a while by muddleheaded sentiment, but in the end they understand and admire hardheaded common sense, and are willing to have proposals and ideas discussed critically back and forth before action starts. Reaction they despise, but fundamentally they are intelligent conservatives, whether they admit it or not. When it comes to the method of accomplishing the goal, a new social order for instance, they will listen with respect to an intelligent presentation of ways and means. See to it that you give them such a constructive alternative for the cure-alls and nostrums.

THEIR GOAL PROTECTS THEM

So there you are. I have seven of this younger generation at home. They don't pay much attention to me, or so it seems. In the youngest the repetition of discipline shows results finally. But in the older ones—Well, I thought I was persuasive last year, but I discovered recently under the lapel of the last fall's suit of my oldest daughter, eighteen, a Roosevelt button. Or perhaps it is the question, to smoke or not to smoke, in which my opinion seems unimportant. Similar experiences may seem to shake the foundations of our faith now and then, but that is the nature of faith.

Finally after method of reform you come to the question of motive. There and there only have we the great advantage over the promisers. They promise everything for the body and not much for the soul. Even the Church Convention pronouncements for a new economic order are mostly couched in terms of creature comfort. In this lonely passage of each soul through life, the promisers help little. Young people want something spiritually permanent and enduring, a cause to which they can attach themselves. They believe that we are progressing toward a goal, an ideal commonwealth on earth, a city with foundations. And they have a passionate conviction that a moral power working through men in each generation can change that generation for the better.

Faith returns and we know that modern times are solidly built on youth.

CHAPTER FOUR

What Can a Man Do?[1]

ONE CONVENTION OF WHOSE UTILITY I HAVE some doubt is the one which requires that a graduating class, as it leaves its alma mater for the world of affairs, shall listen to a distinguished statesman, or at least a distinguished name, or if all that fails—as it often does despite the efforts of the president—somebody, anybody who will deliver a commencement address.

The conventions are fairly definite as to what one must say—which makes it less important of course how well the distinguished name can speak. I am to lay out for you a philosophy of life, with due emphasis on religion, to guide you down, or up, the pathways of experience to the grave. I must set forth the essentials of democracy, with sly digs at President Roosevelt or the economic royalists, or both, and urge upon you the necessity of deep interest and participation, if possible, in politics and government. I am supposed to rise to the heights of eloquence in denouncing the "isms" of the day. And if I am any good at all I should bring you to your feet cheering, by a peroration that predicts a parliament of man, a federation of the world, all without benefit of entangling alliances for the United States of America.

Can I do all that without boring you stiff, and without repeating what you heard last year and the years before, and what you see during these June weeks in every newspaper you pick up?

DOES DEMOCRACY MEAN ANYTHING?

A very wise man once said that a speech should always answer an important question in the minds of the audience. I wonder what

[1] Talk at Rochester University, Rochester, N.Y., June 21, 1937. Printed in *Vital Speeches of The Day*, 1937.

26

the question is today? "Does democracy mean anything?" is the topic of my address. But I am not sure that such an apparently abstract matter meets the situation here.

I wonder what place in the world of affairs is waiting for each of you? And I wonder what impress each of you will leave on that world? Last year the secretary of the Harvard Class of 1911 gave an answer for his classmates twenty-five years after graduation, of which you may have read. It was none too encouraging. What can a man do? What is his motive-power? What will he be worth to himself and his generation?

There was a day when man was lost in a mass of human flesh that was a machine to build a pyramid. The Christian Gospel made him a personality with the power of God in him, but centuries after he was still cannon-fodder. Perhaps he hasn't lost all characteristics of cannon-fodder yet. But the Puritan revolution aided by the development of modern science started something different. There my story begins.

In 1647, nearly three hundred years ago, Charles I and Cromwell were rapidly drawing near that terrible day when the divine right of Kings disappeared under the headsman's axe.

A committee of the Army of Roundhead Puritans—Baptists, Levelers, and so on—came to Cromwell to protest about the administration of the Army, and Cromwell and Ireton met with them.

On the side of the Levelers was the Christian conviction that in every man is the divine spark that makes his personality unique and important, and gives him a right to be heard. As one of them put it, "The poorest he in England has a life to live, as the richest he." Ireton couldn't see it that way. Only the man with property and a stake in the community could have any of that sense of responsibility that enabled him to share in the government of the community. Could any discussion be more modern? Can each of the 120,000,000 people of this country really share in its government? Should reliefers vote? Are the masses intelligent enough to elect congressmen and senators, to say nothing of governors and mayors and councilmen? Or must we look to a select group, a monolithic party, the best people, or even a divinely inspired leader to give us our legislation, and tell us what is the true will and good of the people, of the ignorant masses.

ADDING UP GOD'S WILL

Cromwell gave the only possible answer in that dilemma. Because every man, said he, feels God speak in his heart, he is indeed entitled to be heard and to be heard with attention and true tolerance. And when there has been thorough discussion with real consideration for the views of each, then the vote of the majority is likely to represent the will of God for the group.

Perhaps you think that answer was obvious and easy. But 140 years later when our Constitution was adopted only one in twenty-five could vote, and every state but one had property requirements for the suffrage. Woman's suffrage is only seventeen years old. So it took nearly three hundred years to achieve Cromwell's ideal so far as voting is concerned, and even now we can hardly be said to have achieved the goal of full and free and tolerant discussion as the basis for voting. But at least officially and for publication and in commencement addresses we agree today that Cromwell was right.

Yes, it is settled in a way, but does it work? I believe that is still a fundamental question that you ought to clear up in your own mind.

Just what is a man worth? Is there something in each human being that we can call a divine spark? It may be obscure or it may be a flame, but do you really believe that from it can come some contribution, large or small, to the life of the community?

That question is at the heart of our industrial problem today. Here is a group of workmen joined with other workmen in the same industry. They can vote for political candidates, and the majority names the winner. As workmen are they any less capable of governing themselves? Do they at once become communists or revolutionists just because they organize into a union and seek to have an organized voice in various matters that concern them? Why should not a majority name the representatives for all? My representative in Congress is a landslide Democrat, and I certainly didn't vote for him, but I have no other representative, for nobody is in Congress for whom I voted. What is the difference?

You say that union leaders are drunk with power and condone violence and racketeering and aren't responsible, and that even where they are all right, they can't manage their men. If that were all true, which it isn't, you could duplicate it all in American political history. Do you believe in men and women and their capacity, or don't you? You had better make up your mind whether you stand with Ireton, or with Cromwell and the Levelers.

PLAYING ALONG WITH "THE BOYS"

I can answer that first question to my own satisfaction, but a second one is more difficult. Can you go into politics and stick to your ideals? Now, I am an idealist, as you have perhaps observed, but I also claim to be a realist. I am no Pollyanna, and I agree with the great Spanish diplomat and statesman Madariaga that an idealist must be a realist or ideals become illusions. The first great realist in politics was Machiavelli who set forth with cynical clarity exactly how a Prince should gain power and keep it. Are all methods justified in order to succeed? To make it quite concrete, do we have to have Jim Farley and spoils in order to have Franklin D. Roosevelt? Is it necessary for the success of the New Deal to quash federal indictments and make peace with Huey Long's successors? Just to make it bipartisan, is it necessary in order to maintain the fundamental patriotic principles for which the Republican party stands, to have the Penrose Quay Vare machine in Pennsylvania or the Cox-Hynicka machine in Cincinnati? Do you have to play along with "the boys" in order to get out the vote for President, overlooking a little local graft and murder because it is only teeny-weeny?

Well, a lot of people do, and you had better make up your mind about your view now. In a tough election like that last fall, "the boys" lose their enthusiasm for your presidential candidate, and may even trade off votes for his opponent to be sure to get their local ticket elected, carrying with it the real jobs and patronage.

But I'm here to tell you that you can have honest local government and you can take part in politics without getting dirt on your hands. If you can do it there, you can do it beyond that in state and national politics. I don't mean that you go around wearing a halo and insulting people. But I do mean that you test policies and programs by sound, honest, common sense, not by some imaginary necessity of the political machine. You have to be diplomatic and tactful, you have to get along with people you disagree with and perhaps disapprove of, but you don't have to sell your soul to anybody for anything.

MACHIAVELLI VS. LINCOLN AT HOME

I recognize that national politics are more difficult to handle. But I don't find much of Machiavelli in Abraham Lincoln. Lincoln was a politician and a shrewd one, and perhaps in his earlier career there might have been some deals subject to ethical criticism. But there is no encouragement to "blood and iron" in his conduct of the Presidency, and I can't think of him somehow as either slick or devious. There was a hardness of steel in him in defense of principles, but certainly neither cruelty, ruthlessness, nor deceit in seeking or retaining power. There was no harshness or indifference to the individual, but on the contrary an inclusive affection for individual men, women, and children that grew from a mystical belief in the equality of men before God, very like that of the Levelers, by the way. He was the idealist in action because he grounded his policy on an almost fatalistic conviction that the right in the end must and would prevail. So far as I am concerned in politics, I vote for Lincoln, not Machiavelli.

Of course, Machiavelli's greatest vogue has been in international affairs. In the religious wars of the sixteenth and seventeenth centuries he was the authority coequal with the Old Testament for murder, burning, and pillage. Gradually there came a change, until today the slaughter of the innocents is at least frowned upon in polite society. But the puzzle still remains. Must a diplomat be at best a liar, and at worst a villain? As a modern political realist puts it: "It is satisfactory to be able to show that if a certain statesman, in dealing with a certain emergency, had acted with less perfidy or inhumanity, or had been somewhat honester or more generous, his adventure would have prospered better than it did. But it is not equally consoling to find, as we sometimes do, that if at the critical moment, he had been more unscrupulous or more violent, or had merely had the sense to wear a mask of deceit, he might have achieved some wise and patriotic purpose, instead of ruining himself and allowing grave injury to befall his country."

AND ABROAD

The statesmen who created a united Italy and a united Germany, essentials of a modern world, were surely disciples of that philosophy. The blood and iron of Bismarck is revived in these days with the same cynical disregard of solemn engagements and contempt for idealism whether expressed as international law or as a League of Nations.

How does one meet that situation? You may think my answer weak, for it depends much on faith. As I read history there is, in spite of ups and downs, a steady progress toward a more ideal commonwealth, national and international. Each generation has it in its power to contribute to that progress. And to paraphrase Daniel Burnham, the great architect and city planner, a noble logical plan for that progress once ably set forth lives on with increasing power.

From a study of that progress in the past, I believe that these dictatorships that threaten our peace today have in them the seeds of their own destruction, and that no outside force from us or any one else can bring the return of democracy any more quickly than it is coming anyhow. I believe that a large measure of that sense of injustice that sustains those dictatorships and breeds war, can be eliminated by peaceful methods. Once more I vote against Machiavelli and his disciples, and for those great souls, the true realists, beginning with Hugo Grotius and ending with Stresemann and Briand and Stimson and Hull, who see the vision of a peaceful commonwealth of nations and use honest means to achieve it.

THE BIG CONTEST

You may think I have wandered a good way from the questions I put at the beginning of these remarks. What place will you fill and what impress will you leave on the world of affairs?

That depends on whether like Cromwell you believe in people. It depends on whether you stick to your ideals, as Henry Bentley and Murray Seasongood did in Cincinnati, and as Lincoln did in Washington. And it depends above all on whether you feel yourself in the stream of history as part of a generation through whom God is trying to work out his purposes.

We don't believe in a personal devil these days, but there is a very great philosopher of the day who finds as the only solution of the problem of the pain and evil we can't help seeing in the world, a revolutionary hypothesis that in the very nature and substance of God himself there may be a contrast, a struggle.

You and I feel that struggle going on within ourselves. In such a contest surely there is only one side on which we want to fight. And so for guides at the commencement of your careers, I give you Cromwell and Lincoln.

CHAPTER FIVE

Thinking versus Swearing in Labor Relations[1]

LABOR UNIONS ARE IMPRESSING THEMSELVES upon the national consciousness in these days for sure. The American businessman is doing plenty of thinking and swearing about his relations with his employees and their representatives. Every man with a job in a factory is learning his rights from the union organizer. Lawyers are getting into labor law and labor negotiations as never before.[2]

On the sidelines sit many more prople, busy with their own affairs, that are directly or indirectly affected by the industrial struggle. And all around and in the middle are the politicians, the "ins," as shepherds of votes and occasionally as umpires, referees, and field judges; and the "outs," as whispering kibitzers. Where is one to get sanity and light from that conglomeration of interest, prejudice, and indifference?

UNIONS ARE HERE TO STAY

Sanity and light begin with facts. Essential fact No. 1, as I see it, is that labor unions are here to stay. You may think that is self-evident, but it is far from that. If you find a reactionary employer,

[1] Talk before State Bar of Michigan, Ann Arbor, Mich., September 18, 1937. Printed in *Vital Speeches of The Day*, 1937.

[2] I was special U.S. Conciliation Commissioner for the Electric AutoLite Company, Toledo and the dangerous threatened strike of the Toledo-Edison Company in 1934, and chairman of the U.S. Steel Mediation Board in the Little Steel Strike in Cleveland, 1937; I represented employers as labor consultant for twenty years, and acted as attorney for the Amalgamated Clothing Workers during a twelve year period prior to the war.

you will probably find he has a conviction that this present period of agitation and organization is a flash in the pan, that another depression will wipe it all out, and that the "good old days" will return as they did after the bitter agitation of the seventies, the nineties, and of 1919.

All I can say is that I don't believe it. Times have changed, the frontier is gone, and exhaustless supplies of immigrant labor are no longer pouring into our country. The old ways of "handling" strikes and labor troubles are on the way out, if not already gone forever.

"ONE EMPLOYEE WAS HELPLESS"

Essential fact No. 2 is that labor organization has been a necessary element in the protection of the interests of the workers.

To prove that is a fact, I need only rely upon the opinions of the Supreme Court of the United States, handed down sixteen years ago in American Steel Foundries v. Tri-City Central Trades Council (1921) 257 U.S. 184, 209:

> A single employee was helpless in dealing with an employer. He was dependent ordinarily on his daily wage for the maintenance of himself and family. If the employer refused to pay him the wages that he thought fair, he was nevertheless unable to leave the employ and to resist arbitrary and unfair treatment. Union was essential to give laborers opportunity to deal on equality with their employer. . . . To render this combination at all effective, employees must make their combination extend beyond one shop. It is helpful to have as many as may be in the same trade in the same community united, because, in the competition between employers, they are bound to be affected by the standard of wages of their trade in the neighborhood.

Most of us, when we think of sweated industries, like the needle trades in the old days, and exploited workers, like girls and women in some types of department stores, restaurants and hand laundries, agree with the necessity for some kind of protection. There are always forward-looking employers who need no regulation by the state, or pressure from a union, to treat their employees like human beings. But, in general, improvement has come through a combination of factory legislation and union organization, or the threat of organization.

SELF-PROTECTION IS DEMOCRATIC

Essential fact No. 3 is that labor organizations are capable of making a fundamental contribution to democracy in industry. Surely if protection is needed, self-protection is best. Remember, in the Commonwealth they put it this way, "The poorest he in England has a life to live as the richest he." That means a life of his own, a full life, a life of opportunity, a life of satisfaction because he is doing necessary work for the community. Today it means wages that give him and his family reasonable comfort and decent surroundings. That is the beginning of democracy, without which it cannot grow.

Democracy means not only wages and hours and working conditions that permit a man to live a decent life of his own, but it means the man has a right to achieve those aims by his own efforts. Benevolent despotism in the political field is something we don't think much of in the United States. Why should we think any more of benevolent despotism in industry? A man has a right to a voice in those matters that affect him in his job.

As a matter of fact all intelligent industrialists who can read the signs of the time have recognized that principle and installed grievance systems, whether their companies deal with their unions or not. Men in plants know they can get a real complaint past the foreman to the management and get some adjustment.

Men today are entitled to bargain collectively with their employers. A right long recognized by the courts is now fully protected by law.

In some cases, nearly always through unions, agreements have been reached setting up tribunals to decide questions about which the men and the management can't agree. And that is a fundamental step in a democracy, the creation of courts of justice. This whole process would hardly have been achieved if labor unions had not existed.

THE STRIKE IS CIVIL WAR

Essential fact No. 4 is that questions have come up even in democracies which could only be settled by civil war. Until we reach an ideal commonwealth, men will always retain the right to strike. But I insist that it is a sign of the breakdown of democracy when we have to have a war to settle anything. The strike, like civil war, ought to be a last resort. It is the last resort of the most experienced and responsible unions, and the sudden walkout, without real bargaining first, is the sign of the incompetent organizer or business agent. So is the sit-down strike, and the union leaders who know their business don't use it. But strikes do come and create conditions that rouse the community to action in its own defense.

That action must be taken by legislation, not by self-help through vigilantes. And that legislation must be adopted in the light of our four essential facts. Its object, of course, must be to prevent strikes, but it ought to have the positive purpose of encouraging democracy in industry. That means not only to promote the democratic process in industrial plants, but also to promote and assist the democratic process in labor unions. There is no sense and no progress in exchanging a benevolent despotism in industry for a benevolent despotism in the operation of a labor union.

DEMOCRACY IN INDUSTRY

Legislation having to do with collective bargaining operates to promote democracy in industry. Workers can organize, and if a majority do organize themselves they speak for the whole.

Workers in organizing can do so without interference from the employers, and organization under his domination is contrary to law. But nothing is said in the Wagner Act about intimidation by fellow employees or other persons, and that is not justice or democracy. Francis Biddle, then Chairman of the old Labor Board, said so in Cincinnati about the NIRA nearly three years ago, but the Administration and Congress paid no attention. The fact that employers have fought unions in the past by discrimination and intimidation is no reason for condoning those practices now on the other fellow's part.

EXPERTS FOR UNION AGENTS

The representatives of employees need not be from their own number. That provision is sound, both because equality in bargaining may require a representative who is not also an employee, and because employees are entitled to expert advice if they want it. But that means that union agents ought to be experts in the business, able not only to talk intelligently about the problems of the men, but familiar with the problems of the business.

When the parties make a deal, it ought to be put in writing. "Collective bargaining" contemplates ending in a bargain, and it would be a good idea to amend the Wagner Act to say so unequivocally, without waiting around for the Supreme Court to pass on ambiguous language. That was not the issue in the steel strike, and even Senator Vandenberg's proposed amendments include such a provision.

SOME THINGS CAN'T BE ARBITRATED

The second important field of legislation is that for preventing and settling trade disputes. Mediation or conciliation is the commonest and most effective way to do that. The Wagner Act makes no reference to mediation, although regional directors of the National Labor Relations Board frequently serve as mediators. The only Federal statute on the subject was passed in 1913, and gives the Secretary of Labor power to mediate or to appoint commissioners of conciliation. They have no power to subpoena witnesses or to take testimony, although state laws often give their corresponding officials those powers. The federal statutes should do the same.

There are no compulsory arbitration laws in the United States, and no laws are necessary of course for voluntary arbitration. Arbitration, however, is unpopular, because both parties feel that it is likely to end by splitting the difference, and they could compromise on that without paying an arbitrator. If the issue is a closed shop or recognition of the union, it can't be arbitrated.

One other scheme is in force in Canada and Colorado which seems to have much merit, although it has not spread elsewhere. Those states provide that it shall be illegal to strike unless application has been made for a board of investigation and a certain number of days allowed to pass for it to make a report. In most cases these boards do not investigate, but try to bring the parties together by mediation, and they have been remarkably successful in preventing threatened strikes. Of course some strikes they cannot settle, and a certain number of strikes take place illegally before the period is up, or even without application for a board. Study indicates, however, that these illegal strikes are generally in depressed industries like lumber and coal.

PRIVATE ARMIES

When strikes do take place the whole community often has to face the fact of violence. I am not talking about a little hairpulling or shin-kicking on the picket line, or even a good fist-fight around the corner. I am referring to organized intimidation and even killing, and I feel just as strongly about private armies as I do about mass picketing. Mayor LaGuardia put it as well as anyone: "Regardless of one's views, when force is used to exact any demand improperly or illegally, a superior force must be used to suppress it. On the other hand, the Police Department belongs to all the people and not to any one group. The policemen's nightstick must not be used to settle economic issues."

But the Police Departments need some help in knowing what their duties are. We ought to have rules laid down to govern and strictly to control industrial warfare. Furthermore, the rules ought to be statutory and not judicial, varying with the length of the Lord

Chancellor's foot. And the rules ought to be enforcible by the representative of the public, the county prosecutor or the attorney-general, and not in a private action by one of the parties to the dispute.

RULES OF WARFARE

The first subject to be covered is the definition of a legal strike. The legislature ought to say for instance whether it is legal to strike for a closed shop, and end this anomaly by which in all states it is legal to make a closed shop contract with a union, but illegal in most for a union to strike for a closed shop. The legislature ought to lay down the requirements for a valid employment contract and outlaw those contracts by which an employee on hourly pay is apparently tied up for some definite period, although the employer is not bound to give him any minimum amount of work.

The statute should define legal picketing as nearly as that can be done, of course forbidding violence, and lay down some reasonable criterion for the number of pickets in proportion to the number of workers in the struck plant. It ought to forbid intimidation and give it some definition, applied both to the place of employment and to the homes of employees.

Your Michigan bill which was vetoed was certainly a great step forward in one respect, for the old rule that all picketing was illegal is a relic of feudalism. But the effort to restrict pickets to employees was directly in conflict with the views of the Supreme Court of the United States in the American Steel Foundries case, which I quoted a few moments ago. Referring to picketing by outsiders—members of unions whose trades were involved in the strike—the Court said:

They may use all lawful propaganda to enlarge their membership, and especially among those whose labor at lower wages will injure their whole guild. It is impossible to hold such persuasion and propaganda, without more, to be without excuse and malicious.

THE UNION WITH CHARACTER

Much of the discussion of industrial strife in the last few months has included demands for legislation to make unions responsible. But responsibility is just another word for character, and character cannot be created by law either in unions or in employers. Incorporation is often referred to. But incorporation does not add to responsibility. It makes it a little easier to sue and get service, but it limits the liability of members.

Furthermore, the responsibility of unions is individual. They vary like people, and their character does not depend on affiliation with the C.I.O. or the A.F. of L. In the C.I.O., you have the Amalgamated Clothing Workers, the United Mine Workers and the Typographical Union, every one of which has an outstanding record for responsibility. In the A.F. of L., you have the Pressmen, the Railway Clerks, and the Electrical Workers with equally good records. Outside of either fold are the other railroad brotherhoods, the aristocracy of labor so-called. Those unions have achieved responsible character by experience. Others in the C.I.O. and the A.F. of L. have not yet reached that point. Legislation, therefore, should be aimed at helping sound leadership to develop with democratic methods.

THE BRITISH WAY

The best solution, I believe, is that suggested by English experience. The key to that experience lies in the granting of certain privileges and exemptions to trades unions if they will register and comply with certain requirements. Registration is not compulsory but nearly all unions register, because the privileges are substantial and the requirements are not burdensome, but on the contrary somewhat helpful. They refer principally to regular reports of financial condition. The privileges and exemptions, you will perhaps be startled to hear, effective since 1906, include freedom from liability for torts, for conspiracy, for restraint of trade, or for causing breach of an existing contract of employment.

I might add by way of footnote that some recent public comments on the severity of English legislation against unions are quite inaccurate. Illegal picketing is defined in England and this criminal law is enforced by the police, seldom if ever by injunction. Certain strikes are illegal; those in sympathy with a strike in a different trade or industry (which are rare anyway); or a strike designed to coerce the government directly or by inflicting hardship on the community (that is, a general strike, which is equally rare). Political contributions are allowed, but only from funds to which union members subscribe individually and specifically.

English unions are of course liable for breach of contract, but so also are American unions, and neither incorporation nor any other statute could make them any more so, except perhaps by making service on a local union operate as service on the national union.

TOWARD REAL LABOR PEACE

The application of that English experience to the United States would involve the granting of certain exemptions to labor unions, like those in the Norris-LaGuardia Act,[1] upon registration with the state or federal government. Registration might require regular financial statements, and set up protections to the democratic process as desired by the best thought of the unions themselves. That is no cure for irresponsibility, but it would help.

There are the broad lines of a labor policy, but no labor policy can bring peace except through the persons involved as employers and employees.

As I observe the American scene, there has been a great change in the attitude of employers in the last twelve months. Most of them opposed the Wagner Act, but, especially after the decision of the Supreme Court, they have taken the proper attitude for a citizen of democracy, that it is the law and ought to be obeyed. They have been willing to deal with unions; they have been dis-

[1] The Norris-LaGuardia Act was passed in 1932, and signed by President Hoover. For all practical purposes it eliminates injunctions in the Federal Courts in connection with strikes or labor boycotts.

tressed and worried by the inexperience of some union leadership; they have come to realize their own inexperience, and they are trying in good faith to promote peace in industrial relations. I suggest that our profession can have no higher aim during these next years than to seek that same end. We can avoid technicalities, get down to fundamentals, and promote real collective bargaining.

CHAPTER SIX

The Rock of Our Salvation[1]

$\mathcal{A}$ LITTLE OVER A HUNDRED AND FIFTY years ago Gibbon finished writing the *Decline and Fall of the Roman Empire*. What he wrote in his autobiography about that thrilling moment sounds a little like thoughts on a commencement: "I will not dissemble the first emotions of joy on the recovery of my freedom and perhaps the establishment of my fame. But my pride was soon humbled, and a sober melancholy was spread over my mind, by the idea that I had taken an everlasting leave of an old and agreeable companion."

So this morning you all share the sobering thought of a parting with the stability of this institution, and you of the graduating class share the still more disturbing conviction that you will never be together again. But the joy of freedom after accomplishment and the eager and searching gaze toward a future of successful living quickly rises above any note of melancholy and regret.

Thus the commencement orator establishes the justification for his selection, by displaying his keen understanding of the psychology of youth, while lightly tossing off an apt reference from the classics (for the faculty), and gently striking a note of sentiment (for the parents).

Having in this way secured the attention of his audience, the orator must proceed to set up a few guideposts for the eager young souls before him, so soon to start on the highway of life, in terms suitable for future quotation by the clergy and other budding commencement orators present.

If it were only as simple as that! To commencement orators who will be sounding off for two weeks now, I commend the remark of

[1] Fiftieth Commencement Address, Bryn Mawr College, June 7, 1939.

William Morris about people engaged all about us in making others live lives which are not their own, while they themselves care nothing for their own real lives.

Yet I am charged with the task of a commencement oration. My solution is to discuss with you for a few minutes the problem that has grown increasingly fascinating to me over the twenty-one years since my own class would have graduated. If you find my ideas helpful, you are welcome to them, but having some slight experience of seven children, God forbid that I should recommend to you any life but your own.

HOUSE OF OUR DAYS TO COME

Where are we to find security? Is it in those elements that make a good living—a job, a house, a family and social life? or is there something more to be added, something by way of religion? What is the rock of our salvation? to use the old phrase from the Psalms. What foundation shall we use for the house of our days to come?

Twenty-one years ago, instead of attending my own Commencement, I was in the Army and in France, an enlisted man at an officers' school. I had put in a year with a regular Army regiment of the Second Division and learned the attitude of the old-timer. There was no use worrying or being bored. As long as we had American rations instead of British or French, we had plenty chow. Beds were good enough most of the time. Like the great majority of American doughboys, we didn't have much of the front line. Even for those that did, "the sanctity and importance of sudden death was a comforting and salutary thing, a last little rock, as it were, in the shifty sands." Three squares and a flop stood for a security that the boys began to appreciate when after an honorable discharge they set out to look for a job.

CHOW AND A ROOF FOR ALL

For the great majority of boys and girls who like you are ending their education, that kind of security is no objective to be sneered at. Many of you here have definite ideas for your future, ranging from an immediate partnership with some fortunate young man, to a somewhat more prosaic occupation—a job of your own. Not that the first alternative may not be a job, too.

Many more of you will return to your homes and become simply receptive, waiting for life to unfold. You have security on a glorified Army model. Only a few of you need to be disturbed about the continued provision of three meals and a place to sleep, but you few are far more typical of the youth of our country as they march out this month into the existing economic system. Man shall not live by bread alone, but he does need bread, and many can find no way to earn it.

Many more fortunate people today are deeply concerned about the situation of that other one-third of the nation which is ill fed, ill clothed, and ill housed. Every large city has organized its socially minded citizens to plan an attack on these deficiencies. The family welfare societies, the child care agencies, the health federations, hospitals, and clinics have been joined by public agencies including those for public support of the unemployed; and finally the government has stepped in to influence the basic elements required for recovery, by efforts at national planning of production.

BEYOND THREE SQUARES AND A FLOP

Beyond all that is an ideal of a community in which there shall be a chance for every child to grow up healthy, strong, intelligent, not only able but entitled to make his contribution to the common good. A decent house, a job, a social life worth living, with recreation, educational opportunities, art, and music, are part of the completed picture.

The achievement of that ideal lies through thorny problems like banking and credit, prices, wages, and monopoly, tariff and exchange controls, balance between agriculture and industry, purchasing power against durable goods, employer and employee relations. So we social reformers find ourselves, with businessmen and politicians, over our heads in economics, obsessed with statistics, drowned in sociology. Theology is a matter for antiquaries.

OVER OUR HEADS IN ECONOMICS

That is the culmination of a long development. Nearly one hundred years ago a man taught by Hegel denied his master, and insisted that ideals were simply the reflection in the human mind of the material world. Karl Marx held that the real forces controlling historical development in all its phases were to be found in the reaction upon the behavior of man of the economic position he occupies. Ideas don't create a culture; the practical methods of production and its physical and cultural conditions determine the whole cultural order of an epoch—moral, religious, social, and political. That much of Marx we seem to have swallowed whole. Our obsession today is with the methods of production. We cry for action and more action to improve those conditions and to discover what interferes with the proper operation of the methods, expecting like Marx that with success in that effort, all our ideals will be added unto us. We are certainly not socialists today in any sense that would satisfy Marx, but his economic deteminism has conquered us after ninety years, and economics has become to most of us the rock of our salvation.

Don't think that I am attacking the ideal of the full dinner pail, and the clean solid house. Neither am I suggesting that we abandon the effort to solve our economic problems. I am simply raising the question of priorities; whether a glorified three squares and a flop with all the frills is the standard by which we are to measure community success, or whether there is some other standard of values that we need to be studying while we push along the highway?

Very likely you may suggest that of course you believe in religion and spiritual values, but that they cannot live in the slums and on relief and in sweat shops. Therefore you say we must first attack these inequalities and injustices. Yes, it is to some degree a matter of emphasis. But I am a pragmatist and I am guided a good deal by the way the thing works when you seek first the kingdom of economics and expect all else to be added.

WHEN KULAKS AND RELIEFERS AREN'T PEOPLE

Marx's principles won out in Russia and that ought to serve as some sort of a testing ground. I realize that there the church had been the tool of a reactionary state, and created in the revolutionaries a hatred of organized religion, just as the state church in Germany had produced the same hatred in Marx. Of course also the Russians were never an industrial nation and they had a long way to go to get their standard of living up to any kind of decent level. But my test is in the way they treat people. I can understand a wartime psychology toward kulaks and White Russians. But when you reach the point where you permit three million innocent Ukrainians to starve because you need their wheat to get cash to buy machines, that seems to me some evidence that there needs to be something added to an economic plan to make it a rock upon which to base our salvation. I submit that the effort in Russia to build a state capitalism without belief in God is what produces the cruelty to man and the disregard of personality that most observers report. So for Germany, where even the fanatical nationalism is likely to be in material terms, that is, associated with a superhumaniim.

Come closer home. Do you find anything to be proud of in our attitude toward reliefers? Never such interest in economics. Never, I think, such disregard of human misery. The administration presses appropriations for three million on W.P.A., but washes its hands of two million desperate or despairing people on local relief who get half the W.P.A. allowance per family per month. And many of the 85 per cent in our cities who are not on relief or W.P.A. complain of chiselers and really believe reliefers are bums and won't work. Some are like that, but most of them are ordinary people in trouble, treated like dirt.

ECONOMIC FATALISTS

Vhat is lacking is belief in people and their capacity, belief that every last one of them has some bit of the divine spark if you'll give them a chance to show it. It is a curious paradox that this tremendous interest in economic reform should be found side by side with a distrust of those who are to benefit by it. Distrust of people shows itself these days in a good many ways besides the attitude toward reliefers. The vigorous reforming preacher makes Sam Insull his whipping boy. The President picks out the Liberty League and businessman X . . . or was it Y? Otherwise sane people light on the communists. Businessmen talk about the brain trust. The National Association of Manufacturers won't believe that their employes can be intelligent enough to choose an honest business agent. All of us damn politicians—except the commencement orator who claims to be one.

A few weeks ago I was in a small group with a high administration official, where we were discussing the elements necessary to restore employment. The government man said little, but did make this one revealing statement: "Suppose the Republicans win in 1940 and all excuse for want of confidence is removed. How much capital investment can business put into the economic system? Not more than two billion dollars, and that is no more than government is putting in now. Then how can we expect business to do this job from here on?" That is substantially the position of the seven economists whose recent book has had such a vogue.

Now the cardinal sin of a commencement orator is to make a political speech, but surely I may be permitted to point out that the seven economists, like Marx, are economic fatalists and have no confidence whatever in those intangibles that we call the spirit of man.

I repeat that I don't mean to overlook the economic elements. I mean simply that you can't ignore the spiritual elements either. A football team wins over a team equally good or better, sometimes by luck, but more often by something intangible in the men who make the team. Chinese and Japanese do things with the soil, because teeming millions are jammed into a small space, that even the A.A.A. would say was impossible, if they didn't know it had been done.

We are accustomed in these days to the atmosphere of crisis.

It is in foreign affairs, or in labor relations in the coal mines, or in the communist menace, or in the British Ambassador's tea for the King and Queen. But we can't sustain the excitement and we grow thick skinned, cynical, restored to self-attention.

That in itself it seems to me is a spiritual crisis. Marxian socialism or communism will never get far in this country, but the economic fatalism and the denial of any but material ideals, which are the essence of Karl Marx, have come pretty close to capturing us, intellectuals, politicians, businessmen.

Are three squares and a flop the rock of our salvation?

BEYOND BREAD—WHAT?

Certainly they were not equivalents to the Psalmists. He was talking about God, a moral being that gave strength and health to men in distress and preserved them for his service. He was the shadow of a great rock in a weary land.

Our economic experiences are not so new. Amos raged at men that falsified their balance, that sold the needy for a pair of shoes. He was prepared to take the women of Israel, in high Samaria, whom he called the Cows of Bashan, lolling on their ivory divans, and haul them out with fish lines and hooks.

Habakkuk described that bitter and hasty nation that marched through the breadth of the land to possess the dwelling places that were not theirs, which was terrible and dreadful; which came all for violence, which scoffed at kings and derided every stronghold.

It was not the economic determinists of those days, the businessmen or politicians, or even the eager young students, who preserved that ancient core of our religion. It was a remnant of faithful men and women of the ancient Hebrews who carried it through the Exile and made the Jewish nation. It was the successful passage through every kind of spiritual strain known to man that taught that unknown seer to write:

They that wait upon the Lord shall renew their strength; they shall mount up with wings as eagles; they shall run and not be weary; and they shall walk and not faint.

In other words it was a religion that worked.

Sir Josiah Stamp has shown how in the time of Christ there existed economic conditions not so different from some of ours, with a few wealthy and a great mass on the edge of poverty and distress, barely able to sustain themselves much of the time.

So Christ's teaching of the New Testament was the resultant of the ancient reformers, the great burning preachers, and the newer editors, drawn through a mind of simplicity and power, cast in an atmosphere of love and affection for men, women, and children, and all set in an economic background nearly as desperate as any-thing Marx and Engels could paint—if you chose to look at it that way. He didn't.

He even faced a totalitarian state, and was crucified by it. He failed, but in three hundred years he captured the Roman Empire.

IS THAT RELIGION RELEVANT TODAY?

Can it be still the rock of our salvation?

The fact that it has endured for two thousand years is some evi-dence. It has cast up many figures, like that of Francis of Assisi, which are certainly worthy to stand with any in the Bible. And thousands and millions of your ancestors and mine have found comfort and strength and health that made it worth while to earn a living however great the hardships.

The accomplishments of our religion are a little more definite than that. Three hundred years ago the Commonwealth men whipped Charles I and sat down to decide what form the new constitution should take. The Radicals were for manhood suffrage, for, said they, God speaks to each man without the intervention of a priest, and each man has a right to say what is God's will for him. That includes how he shall be governed. Ireton for Cromwell asserted in reply that to give every man a vote would mean that those without property would outvote those with property, and then take it away from them. That in other words was commun-ism; and how modern it all sounds. It is indeed the beginning of modern politics. From the Restoration on losing an election no longer meant losing your head.

What brought the change? It can be traced I think in substantial part to the Methodist and Baptist revivals, the influence of men and women who insisted that there was a God, that all men were his children and deserved to be treated as such. Certain it is, that democracy can only exist while we look on each man, woman, and child as a person, a child of God, who in some degree can make his contribution to the common good. What security is there for our cherished institutions when you begin to think of people as a mass of sheep subject either to the propaganda of the clever, or the kindly ministrations of the wise?

Hegel conceived of the divine and fatherly *Führer*, and Marx of the dictatorship of the proletariat, each feeling that the masses had to be forced into the mold of their ideal, willy nilly. Hegel gave us Russia of the Czars, and Germany of Hitler. Marx gave us Stalin. I prefer Rainborough and his "poorest he in England" who had a life to live, his own, not somebody else's plan for him.

Of course he can't live it in a vacuum. It must be in a community, and the community conditions his freedom. But it involves the slow process of debate and discussion and tolerant listening and persuasion, and compromise.

A PLAN TO WORK ON

That difference and the sole basic difference between the dictatorship and the democracy lies not in their economics, but in the religion of a minority—their belief in God and his power working through individual men and women. The trend toward centralization of authority and responsibility and initiative in Columbus or Harrisburg or Washington is wrong—not because it is Democratic or Republican or New Deal, but because it shows a lack of faith in people, and therefore in God. A city has corrupt utility franchises or a corrupt police force. Let's put the police force under the Governor, say the leaders in Kansas City. Let's put the utilities under a state commission, says Ohio and most other states. But the attitude is wrong, eternally wrong. New York can manage its own police; why not Kansas City? Cincinnati can manage its utility franchises; why not the other cities? Certainly we need legislation in Ohio to regulate the utilities, better legislation than the utilities have let us have up to now. We may even need the federal law, because our utility buys its gas at the Kentucky state line, from a cousin subsidiary, to be sure, but still from a different corporation, and Ohio can't control that. But we need to place the responsibility for self-government and self-control on the smallest unit where the job can be adequately done. We need faith in people and faith in God who works in them.

Our religion is simple enough. It lays down two great commandments from Exodus and Leviticus. Thou shalt love the Lord thy God, and thy neighbor as thyself. There are the principle of leadership and the principle of community, which Hitler and Stalin and Mussolini have seized upon and perverted.

But it says to the individual something a little different, and never with more force than to a graduating class. Here is a gospel of perfection, perfection in your own life, and perfection for your community from class to world stage. God knows we are far from that perfection in both respects, and if we look on that gospel as something like a set of laws or a moral code, we can't be much but hopeless lawbreakers.

But if you look at that glorious teaching as a vision to achieve, a plan to work on, a goal and purpose for our own lives and for the life of the race it has a fascination that is deathless from generation to generation. It does not ignore economics, but it says, Seek ye first. There surely is the Rock of our Salvation.

CHAPTER SEVEN

Monday-to-Saturday Religion [1]

I WAS INTENDED THIS EVENING TO TALK learnedly, as an expert perhaps, about college students and their ideas of religion. Well, frankly, I don't know much about it. I have three college students in my own family, one a graduate of a year, one senior, and one freshman. How should I know anything about them?

No, the only higher education I can discuss intelligently is my own, and I can only suspect that if reflections on my own experience are well conceived, they may shed light on the character of present college students and their religion.

I started formal education in religion at an Episcopal Sunday School. There I learned something of Bible stories, but very little about the Bible. I became familiar with the Episcopal service, at least as far as the sermon, but I really didn't learn it until I was in the choir at secondary school.

I was evangelized rather vigorously in my last years at school, with two sessions at the Northfield summer conference, but I didn't quite like it. I would say that a considerable portion of "good citizens" at both school and college felt a distortion of emphasis which lessened the natural appeal of Christian idealism.

With some of my college class after graduation, a sort of instinctive approval of righteousness kept them receptive to religion, and contact through family memberships or the enterprise of attractive pastors related them to the church, probably for the duration.

---

[1] Talk before the Church Society For College Work, General Convention of the Protestant Episcopal Church, Kansas City, Missouri, Oct. 19, 1940.

HIT-OR-MISS RELIGIOUS EDUCATION

But isn't all that a pretty casual kind of religion, almost incidental in its effects on a college community? And what continuity is there between the campus and the home town, to make that religion effective? Can that Christianity be called a design for living for all of us when so little importance is given to it? Was it the dynamic of life for more than a few? Was its relation to the life of the community after graduation made clear at all?

And aren't those questions doubly emphasized when a public institution must forswear religion officially, and make it seem like an extra-curriculum activity, far less important than football or fraternities?

Of course, even twenty-five years ago Christianity was preached to us often as a social gospel. There was religion in Raymond Robbins' story of a fight for clean politics in Chicago. We went six miles to Waterbury after school to spend a weekly evening as volunteer leaders in a city Boys' Club, and the same thing happened in New Haven. The tremendous appeal of remaking the world reached us in vigorous presentation, and reform of business and politics carried the loyalty of the vast majority. But where was the iron needed for the souls of men who could accomplish that? What fire grew in Christianity as presented to us, or even what intellectual and intelligent effort?

MORALS WITHOUT FIRE

In twenty-five years a great deal has happened, but as I see it all these events, war, depression, unemployment, prosperity, depression, unemployment and war again, have only made clearer and more distinct the shortcomings of those of us who stand for Christian idealism. It is not college students we need to talk about in this Church Society for College Work—it is ourselves. Whatever criticism is leveled at them should be turned instead on us. We are their parents, but even more important, we are the makers of their world, both their college world and the vast outside world that surrounds it. If they have no Christianity that can set the world on fire, it is because we have given them none. If we have given them none, we must suspect that we haven't quite the genuine article ourselves, because the real thing is and always has been electric with vitality. The world needs that fire, that electricity today and surely one of the purposes of higher education is to make us more capable of conducting it to the places and the problems that need its inspiration. But how far are we training our children to act in the world of life and reality? We are schooled to believe in courage, in endurance, in honor and honesty. But nobody gave me any help at all in knowing what to do or what to believe in the face of entrenched evil, or wrong before which everyone seems helpless, or pain and suffering that seems so unnecessary.

MONDAY TO SATURDAY TOO

I am not making an easy criticism or suggesting an easy remedy. I want to present the central problem—at least what ought to be the central problem—of Christianity in its relation to higher education, that is, the problem of reconciling the life of us laymen as we live it and think we have to live it each week day, with the perfection of God enjoined upon us by Jesus. If Christianity is a world religion, it ought to give us a realistic philosophy of living, a way of life—and I mean life in an office or factory or store from Monday to Saturday, not just a mushy sentimental perfectionism for Sunday.

Here is a person confronted by a tremendous technical problem— the political management and leadership of a movement for good city government, faced by a powerful political machine; the reorganization of a business flat on its back, competing with unscrupulous opponents; the sound operation of a great children's hospital with a serious financial problem and an apathetic public; the conduct of the foreign affairs of a great democratic nation in a world of force and dictatorship. Are you going to give him any help by saying that if only we can make everybody a Christian, or convert the Dictator, all these problems will solve themselves? It gives no help, and it is not true. Technical problems generally involve problems of personality or personnel, and Christianity in the souls of the people concerned is a powerful solvent. Conversion won't solve technical problems, but it may furnish the dynamic for people who can solve them, so we believe. We say that individuals can get the fire and the guts they need to solve all or any of these problems, only from our Master. But Christianity is not demonstrating that belief or its truth very effectively today. In fact, the preachers don't often analyze at all the relation of dynamic spirit, and technical problems, and the demonic powers.

ECONOMICS LEAVES OUT HUMAN DYNAMIC

We laymen need to know about that. We need to know how to behave when we seem to be faced with alternative courses of action, and they are all bad. We need intelligent instruction about God's progress in history, against the Powers of the Height and of the Depth. We need foundations, even footholds, from which to rise toward the goal we hear about.

Instead we are likely to get, especially perhaps in college, an overwhelming preoccupation with the material bases of life, and that I conceive to be our most profound danger today. Let me illustrate by describing some more or less widely accepted interpretations of our own history and of the apparently dominating figures in that history.

The year before I went to college there was published *The Economic Interpretation of the Constitution.* This was its thesis, substantially in Professor Beard's language. Suppose you were to get the economic biography of the men who made or opposed our Constitution, those who voted for the state legislatures, the legislators themselves who voted for or against ratification, the members of the Constitutional Convention, probably 160,000 in all. This biography would include their lands, houses, loans, capital invested, slaves, state and continental securities. If all the owners of property and their financial associates were for the Constitution, and all the non-slaveholding farmers and debtors against it, then wouldn't that demonstrate that the Constitution was the product of economic interests, that the direct impelling motive of its supporters was the economic advantage which they thought would accrue to themselves?

That thesis is widely accepted today. The method of analysis, which Professor Beard called scientific, is often accepted as such. Because Madison, a keen and responsible politician, wrote that the possession of different kinds and amounts of property divided society into interests and parties, Beard claims that Madison sustains his position.

In 1848 another political scientist wrote:

> The middle class . . . has left no other tie between man and man than naked self-interest, than callous "cash payment." It has drowned the most heavenly ecstacies of religious fervor, of chivalrous enthusiasm, of Philistine sentimentalism, in the icy waters of egotistical calculation. It has resolved personal worth into exchange value.

That interpretation of history is familiar to you. It also is widely accepted.

Another similar interpretation may be less well known. A book was published a few weeks ago which restated in forceful terms the theory that the Civil War was not a war for union, or against slavery, or even a war led in the North by Abraham Lincoln. It was a revolution by which the too slowly growing Northern industrial capitalism asserted its control of the instrumentalities of the national state, and threw out the Southern planter capitalists who thwarted it, and who had been themselves driven into the war by Southern extremists under heavy economic pressure. You may smile, but that is only because this interpretation is not yet established.

THE GREAT DEBUNK

One of the most popular pastimes of recent biographical effort has been the debunking of the lives of the great business and industrial leaders of the years from the Civil War to the turn of the century. We have been gradually persuaded that these robber barons, and their associates the politicos, are the ones who made the amazing progress of the United States in those thirty years. Only this week comes a similar attack on the president-makers.

In the summer before I went to Yale the World War began, and in two and one-half years we were in it. Now most of the people of the United States, even many of those who have changed their minds in recent weeks about our existing situation, believe we were pulled into that first world war by a combination of selfish British and French propaganda, and the economic interests of their most eager tools and associates in this country, our own international bankers and munition makers. We are completely satisfied with the truth of Benjamin Franklin's aphorism that there never was a good war or a bad peace. At the same time we damn the Treaty of Versailles as a plot of the selfish empire-makers, who pulled the wool over Woodrow Wilson's eyes.

I suppose you can see the threads extending through all these interpretations. Man, it is asserted in every kind of language, is dominated by his economic interests, the individual man by the way he earns his daily bread, through the current methods of production, and all of us by governments whose conduct is determined by the profit-seeking of the ruling class, while they fool us with fine phrases. That is the philosophy of Marx and Engels from whom I quoted anonymously a few moments ago, but is it Christian? Or for that matter, is it true?

ECONOMIC DETERMINISM IS BAD HISTORY

That is a question which is not rhetorical. It is a question which we Christians need to face with intelligence and determination. We are natural cynics about others, and especially about our politicians and prominent citizens. We are eager to believe the worst—about others.

That is bad enough, but we go farther and without any intelligent analysis accept an interpretation of history and of current events, and of human nature in politics, which is the reverse of scientific, and in fact denies the fundamental tenets of our religion.

Why do we do it? Well, we look at evil about us—one-third of a nation ill clad, ill housed, ill fed—and we burn with anger at such suffering, so extreme in its contrasts, so unnecessary in an intelligent world. We don't seek or recognize our own personal responsibilities, or the profound difficulty of the readjustments, and we look for a scapegoat, a devil, all red with a tail. But nobody is like those scapegoats of ours. Motives are not all white and all black, nor are they single and simple. We are just kidding ourselves, and probably exhibiting a defense mechanism.

The economic determinism of Beard is bad history, just as bad as the sweetness and light of Parson Weems and the Cherry Tree, which it replaced.

Suppose, to follow Mr. Beard's method, you took the fifty or more richest men in the thirteen states in 1787. Could they have written the Constitution? Having dealt with many businessmen, including the richest, in political matters, I can assure you without even knowing who the fifty were that their experience does not qualify them. Or suppose a selection of property owners at random, or by a Gallup cross section; they couldn't do it either. Even a random selection of property owners down the century and a half since then, couldn't have written it.

Clearly the members of the Convention were able to write the Constitution, first because they were politicians; more than that because they were realistic political scientists of a high order; and even more because they were political idealists. It wasn't their property that qualified them for the job. Is it scientific then, to determine the "immediate guiding purpose" of those men by an analysis of their property?

Besides, we know a great deal about some of those men. They were public men whose acts were nearly all exposed to public gaze. Was Madison a profiteer, or Hamilton for that matter? Are we to waive, as Beard does, the fact that they predicted benefits for the very groups that bitterly opposed the adoption of the

Constitution, and denied any prospect of benefits, and waive the fact that the benefits were in due time realized? Of course, as keen politicians, they appealed to economic motives as well as to patriotism, but even that does not prove the thesis.

THE TENET OF PERSONALITY

We claim to be Christians, and being a Christian to my mind means believing in the worth and importance of individual personalities. Can we permit ourselves to be pulled by our enthusiasm for reform and our hatred of evil into an economic determinism no different in any essential character from the dialectic materialism of the "Communist Manifesto"? Do you believe that the middle class in this country of ours, to which most of us belong, has left no tie between man and man except the cash nexus, and lives in an icy and egotistical calculation? I can't find any word of Jesus that justifies that attitude.

Was Lincoln the dupe of Northern industrial capitalists? What but a perverted reasoning from premises already determined could draw that conclusion? He did all he could to promote industrial production of war supplies. He favored a transcontinental railroad and helped put the legislation for it through a reluctant Congress. But what jaundiced reading of the voluminous record could make that gaunt figure a tool of the interests? I am no blind hero worshipper. I insulted a great admirer of Lincoln at a Rotary luncheon once because my address pictured him as a failure at forty, and a man whose character grew under strain from mediocrity to mastery. No one in his senses can deny the existence of economic motives in all of us, but they are not the ones that give the final answer; they are not the ones that built the United States of America.

Wickham Steed describes a visit to Paris in 1893 and a debate he heard between LaFargue, the son-in-law of Marx, and Jaurès, the great French socialist leader. This very question was the subject of the debate. Let Steed tell the story:

With great eloquence and passion, Jaurès contended that while economic stress had, a various times, played a great part in historical changes, those changes had been prepared and carried through mainly by the spiritual influences such as the conception of justice and freedom, and had, in different ways and degrees, inspired men to struggle for the realization of their ideals.

LaFargue replied by insisting upon the materialist view of history, and by claiming that idealism or religion had been a cloak for the realities of economic strife. . . . He boasted that Marx turned God out of history. . . . The phrase fell flat and Jaurès carried the audience. It is a curious commentary . . . that when LaFargue and his wife felt the approach of age they divided their fortune into so many amounts to be expended annually and, as soon as the last had been spent, they committed suicide. Jaurès remained a leader of French social and political thought, with growing influence and power, until, on the eve of the War (in 1914) he fell a victim to the bullet of a reactionary fanatic.

I would add that his survival might have changed the course of the War and the peace treaty.

SETTING UP SCAPEGOATS

Take the other phase of this materialist thinking that shows through all this reading of our history. You will agree perhaps with what I have said in denying the materialist interpretation of the past. But a suspicion of persons in places of power, a belief that things are run in concealed conspiracy by a few for their own benefit, a disposition to set up prominent persons, or ex-prominent persons, or identifiable groups, as scapegoats, to be blamed for everything evil that we don't like—that is also a materialist interpretation of current history that denies the foundation of our religion. I once heard a man whom I regard as a great religious leader pour vitriol on Samuel Insull, as if Mr. Insull were responsible for all our failure to regulate utilities and securities in local and

state government. There was no analysis—in fact no knowledge—
of what Mr. Insull had accomplished or tried to accomplish, or
exactly what he had failed to do that might have protected the
public better. I'm no defender of Mr. Insull, but I don't see that it
did the group that religious leader was addressing anything but
harm to damn him, for it gave them a comfortable feeling that
they shared no responsibility with such a scoundrel. Insull having
been cast out from good society, there was nothing more for them
to do about regulation of utilities and sale of securities to the public.

Christianity does not excuse us from use of our intelligence;
in fact, a belief that men are children of God requires an intelligent
and humane understanding of individuals, even individuals in high
places who misuse their trust; it requires the sort of confidence in
the ultimate capacities of individuals that Jesus showed when he
wrote on the sand.

MARXISTS IN SPITE OF OURSELVES

We are obsessed with economics and economic motives. We are
told that the political equality we once had is meaningless in the
face of economic inequality. We are assured that conditions as they
now exist do not permit youth of the land to have confidence in
American institutions and the American form of government. I
deny it. The philosophy that told us to seek first the kingdom of
God and his righteousness, and that sent us out to love our neighbors as ourselves, is the only philosophy that can overcome
economic inequality. But we have instead accepted uncritically a
universal indictment of men's motives and given ourselves up to the
economic determinism of Karl Marx. The tragedy is that we don't
even know it. If we damn our colleges and the students in them,
we are in fact damning ourselves because we are infected with the
original virus.

But you say Jesus enjoined upon us a war upon these economic
conditions. That is a view that seems to me distorted, almost as
much out of proportion as the preoccupation with economics and
economic motives to which I have been referring.

Jesus grew up intellectually on the Old Testament. He knew, probably by heart, Isaiah and Amos and the other older stories of burning prophetic attacks on social evils. But, to quote Stamp, "He was so preoccupied with the spirit of man that he accepted the rather indefensible economic conditions of his day, and taught the importance of spiritual compensations in place of temporal revolutions that they (his contemporaries) would rather have heard advocated. He did not outline an ideal social system for his own day; still less did he prescribe one for that day, and even less for today."

Yet even if Jesus' teaching about love of neighbor leads us into a righteous war on economic injustice, it should not lead to a black-guarding of human motives, or to a completely disproportionate emphasis on those prominent figures whose motives are concededly objectionable. I have referred to the robber barons of the Gilded Age. Even the Beards say about John D. Rockefeller, Sr. that he brought "science, acumen, and imagination to the creation of material goods and organizing human services to supply the world with useful commodities of a high standard." What more could be said of a businessman? For all the great fortunes there were great risks. "Only one American railway listed on the London Stock Exchange was paying dividends in 1889, and in less than fifteen years more than four hundred companies had gone into bankruptcy, representing two and a half billions in capital"—so the Beards tell us. And they tell us, too, that in the last half of the nineteenth century our population grew faster than any in Western history, that our national wealth grew fivefold. And between our super-Croesuses and all too widespread poverty, "was a middle class of prosperous farmers, professional workers, and small merchants in larger proportion and enjoying a higher degree of material comfort than in any other country on the globe." That is no jungle roamed by the timber wolves of Big Business. And those small people, reasonably honest and law-abiding, community-makers, were the makers of America, not the towering figures that obscure the landscape. Yet the Beards took forty pages to tell the story of

wickedness and a few paragraphs to tell about the little people. A
recent critic put it this way:

> On the one hand, Marx is telling you in *Das Kapital* that a
> certain historic development indispensable for the progress of the
> race, could only have been carried out by capitalism. And on the
> other hand, he is filling you with fury against the wickedness of
> the people who have performed it.

MEN ARE THE STUFF OF DIVINE POWER

I don't care so much about the defense of capitalism, though I
believe in it. Capitalism can take care of itself. I care profoundly
about the state of mind among Christian people which can yield to
this persistent attack upon the motives of men, men in groups, men
in leadership, all men, and in doing so deny their divine capacity
to be the instruments of God's purpose.

Men are slow and men are stubborn. Take that marvelous story
that Paul Kellogg told on the twenty-fifth anniversary of Survey
Associates, the story of the long fight on the twelve-hour day in
steel. It began more than twenty-five years ago. The first books
and the first speech brought denials and suppression. But there were
conscientious men on the inside and reasonable determined men on
the outside. The first attack was on Sunday work and the seven-day
week. Then followed attack on the twelve-hour day, as humanly
indefensible, industrially inefficient. War came and went. A few
independent mills went to the eight-hour day, through intelligent
leadership. Outside industrialists like Owen Young were seen
and convinced, a White House conference held. Victory finally
came because a President who is sneered at and damned today told
the leaders in steel that one of his speeches on his way to Alaska
would be on the twelve-hour day. The announcement of Harding's
death on the front page was accompanied by a small article on the
inside reporting that the Iron and Steel Institute had voted the
forty-eight hour week. And the final picture of that twenty-year
battle is of an industry that found it could learn regard for human

welfare, and crusaders who worked on the finer feelings of rising generations of men.

Men are slow and they are stubborn, but they can be the very stuff of divine power.

For college students we need an appeal to faith in the power of righteousness working through man, an appeal to persistence, to idealism, to work and sacrifice. We need an intelligent appeal, too. Does our own Christianity measure up in our own minds to that test? We can only find out by trying to state our beliefs for our own observation and study.

A LAYMAN'S RELIGION

Let me try then to state a layman's religion that may appeal to laymen, perhaps to students.

Thou shalt love the Lord thy God with all thy strength and mind and heart and soul. Which means a Father who returns your love, who gives you a feeling of strength and goodness out of which you grow. A man wrote recently of his grandparents and parents, six people. A Scotch sea-captain married a Dutch girl from New Jersey and settled in Minnesota, where their daughter went to school. A circuit-rider from Alabama married a girl who watched him go to the Civil War and saw her son go, too, at fourteen. The Alabama boy and the Minnesota girl met in New York and were married. They worked hard, and they were strong and good. They had many children, and one was this writer. He was proud of all of those six, and of the country they had helped to build. It was not ancestor-worship; it was feeling the sap ascend in his veins. Love of God is like that.

Love of God means a confidence in him and in his power and in his children. His power is exercised through his children, weak and sinful though we may be, missing the mark often, but loving him. His progress is through us and he does progress. To say that our sin and failure is inevitable and persistent is to deny his power and his goodness. We can believe in him and we can overcome both sin and failure, because men under his power have done it before us.

Canon Raven describes these men of power before our time as men "sensitive both to God and to their fellows: they are members in a body, finding freedom in its service, freedom which is at once release from self and energy for experiment and growth."

So far many of our spiritual leaders can take us, but only too few supply the steel the Christian's backbone needs. For we laymen must meet suffering in our circle of family and friends, heartrending, inconsolable pain. We know poverty and unemployment, and the way they can corrode some human souls. We face war in all its horror, and face the necessity as responsible citizens to act for the community in that emergency. Evil is here and no religion worth the name can ignore it. No generation of youth and no generation of maturity will march in a Christian army of power unless that problem is answered in a way to challenge their loyalty and their idealism. It is the same problem to which I referred early in this address.

I FOUND AN ANSWER

I have found an answer that satisfies me, but it came to me long after my formal higher education ended, and I had to dig it out—it wasn't presented to me gratis. Perhaps no answer should come any other way.

God is a loving Father and a wise Father. He is no autocrat, no king on a throne. He fosters the growth of his children by letting them learn their own way, and sometimes we fail and miss the way. Then in that failure a Father suffers with his children, and sometimes more than they suffer. His children suffer sometimes beyond their deserts. We cannot answer why, but we can believe that he suffers with them most of all. We believe that because, at an actual moment in history, a Man who was in himself supremely the Father's Spirit, who had shown us the real nature of the Father, suffered that way without deserving it.

That Man challenged us with divine perfection. It wasn't a code of laws he gave us, that makes us criminals when we violate them, and hypocrites when after failure we still go to church for worship.

It was an ideal, a vision, a plan of human relationships, a goal of effort with a pull and fascination like no other. A city plan permits many nonconforming uses, but it gives us a pattern for our progress, changed often to meet new needs, but always a challenge to produce a better plan for the service of men.

"SOMEONE MUST TELL THEM"

We can't expect miracles, except miracles of spirit and power. We can expect work and failure and work again, and always the comfort of feeling that we are shoulder to shoulder with God, drawing up from all the past and all our past the sap of His strength into our veins.

We are going through no new trials. Read your Bible, especially the Old Testament from which Jesus distilled his philosophy. Try the Psalms and the Apocalypses . . . and Habakkuk. This kind of catastrophe has happened before, and the materialists and dictators of those days are dust, and unhallowed dust at that.

So here we are back in the twentieth century with the alarms of war crashing on our ears—a million college students, the cream of our production of men and women, young, eager, ready to go somewhere; but doubtful, confused, questioning the future and all the past, too.

Could there be a greater challenge to an older generation? Don't you believe that the youngsters have no ears to hear or eyes to see! But someone with the conviction of intelligent faith must tell them, and this Society is the most powerful means through which the word can be sent. Give to that million the belief in their fellows. Give them the feeling you and I have of the power that rises in our veins from the Christian lives that have gone before us and made our country what it is. Deny the power of economics or devastation to crush the human soul. Assert that God working in men will overcome the world.

CHAPTER EIGHT

A Christian Choice of Evils: If War Comes [1]

IF WAR COMES WHAT SHALL I DO? I ASSUME that the *Christian Century* is not asking us ten Christians that question to find out what we think about our own capacities. What is wanted is an expression of our attitudes as Christians toward war.

I do have in a limited way an experience of war at first hand. I enlisted in the Twelfth Field Artillery of the Second Division of regulars in May 1917, when I was nineteen. I served in France for a year, and put in a month at the front as sergeant major of a field artillery battalion. It was a quiet sector and I can't claim to have seen much of the horror of war. However, thirteen of my classmates at Yale died in the war, and others as well whom I counted close friends. I was a reserve officer for twenty years until March 1939, but was unable to take any active training during that period and let the commission run out.

My answer to this question is a Christian answer, but my frame of reference is also that of an amateur politician. I cannot help looking at the problem as it would seem through the eyes of the responsible national leader who carries on his soul the welfare of his people and his country. The reader will have to make allowances for that. [2]

THE OLD ARGUMENTS

First, I want to clear the ground by discussing several fixed ideas that seem to me to obscure the real problem.

[1] Published in the *Christian Century*, Jan. 1, 1941.

[2] I must here acknowledge my deep obligation to Leslie Weatherhead, *Thinking Aloud in War Time;* A. D. Lindsay, *Moral Teaching of Jesus;* R. L. Buell, *Isolated America;* F. S. Oliver, *Endless Adventure.*

Some of the feeling against war comes from a horror of death. Of course the snuffing out of a young life, full of possibilities for good, is a shameful waste of talents given for the service of God. The certainty of that kind of result multiplied many times is a sound and forceful argument against war, anywhere, anytime. But death is an experience we must all face, and some Christians may have to choose it before their time. Christ did. And rose again.

We hate war because war is beastly, and the First World War was perhaps the worst. But it is not true that wars have been a progression toward deeper pits of hell. The predictions of the twenties and thirties about the next war have not been borne out when it came. In fifteen months the British have lost 42,000 lives, combatant and noncombatant, compared to perhaps eight times that in the first fifteen months after August 1914. And pretty bad wars, perhaps worse, happened before 1914. Our Civil War was one.

Again, all wars are not futile. The defeat of France last June was not futile, whatever else it was. Neither was the liquidation of Poland or Czechoslovakia. Germany got what it wanted. Certainly Greece's defense and even Finland's were not futile. Our own Revolutionary War was not futile, even in the light of the Tory viewpoint of *Oliver Wiswell*. Neither were the wars of Garibaldi and Cavour for the unification of Italy, nor the wars of Bismarck for the unification of Germany. They had permanent results, mostly good.

Another common argument against our involvement in war is that an inevitable result will be dictatorship, as bad as the one we may be fighting to destroy. It is true that to wage war today requires an extent of government control in a united effort which makes something close to a voluntary dictatorship. That probably accelerates existing tendencies toward centralization, and perhaps even toward state capitalism. But the real democracies, of three centuries' standing, have gone through and come out of many wars in the last hundred years, and no permanent dictatorship has developed yet.

WE WERE NOT TRICKED

Another widely held view among those who oppose any war under any circumstances is that we were tricked into the last war by a combination of munitions makers, bankers and British propaganda. If it is pointed out that the Germans spent $35,000,000 here in propaganda themselves from 1914 to 1917, the answer is that the British were devilishly clever. If you point out that only 15 per cent of our trade with Britain and France was munitions, they say that the merchants of death were powerful politically. If you point out that profits of all manufacturers were bound to be severely limited if we got into the war (and they were!), they cite J. P. Morgan, though the same limitation was certain to apply to his firm, and in fact his business as a foreign government representative was wiped out.

Well, I lived through those days when I was in college, and we were not tricked. We should probably have made our peace aims a condition of our entrance into the war, but the peace aims were what we fought for and nearly achieved. We did analyze the propaganda and we came to the right decision as between the Allies and Germany before we went in. England and France had made secret commitments with which we could not agree on principle, but even so they were still fighting for something high and fine, something far better than the war aims of Germany. We were fighting for ideals, and the claim of trickery can lead only to a repudiation of ideals altogether, or an insistence that ideals can never be achieved in Europe. I deny either conclusion.

The picture of simple Uncle Sam duped by European tricksters is carried over to the peace and the Treaty of Versailles. Certainly the treaty had its faults, and certainly we paid for not exacting our price when we came into the war. The reparations demanded were impossible. The assignment of war guilt was only partially true, and completely inadvisable. The Polish corridor was a certain source of trouble. Perhaps the worst error was the effort to divide Europe on the basis of nationality, with no restraint upon nationalism.

But we all believed in it then. At that it might have worked if the plan for a moral organization to limit sovereignty had been made to create a real European community. Even so there was no possibility of war until the Rhineland was refortified in 1936. After all, the major object of the treaty was to prevent war, and if enforced in that respect, it would have done so.

WE TURNED BACK!

But the real explanation of our failure in the war and the peace is that, having put our hand to the plow, we—the United States— turned back. We just lay down and quit. Our influence for peace might have accomplished the dream of centuries. No involvement then could have led us to a worse mess than we are in today.

Finally, today we hear about the war between two imperialisms, even from those who do not follow the Communist party line. How can Christians fail to distinguish between the two, when in one there is complete destruction not only of freedom of speech but of all freedom of the spirit; cruel, avowed baiting of Jews and persecutions of Christians beyond anything known in modern times; a treatment of refugees and some subject peoples that can only be described as sadistic, and a disavowal of all morals and ethics that conflict with the new religion of the state? England has its faults, but none like these.

One of the very fine women of our country says that some new conception of humanity is pushing up through the crust of custom in Germany and Italy and Russia, and that it is in its essence good. Great ideas, we are told, enter into reality with evil associates and with disgusting alliances. That view destroys all moral judgment. The contempt for human personality and the arrogant rejection of moral values, characteristic of the Nazi philosophy, are not in their essence or in any part good. They are evil. It may well be that good will come out of that evil, but if it does, it will be in spite of Hitler, Goering and Goebbels, because God turns their cutting edge to his work, not theirs. That does not put them on any wave of the future.

JESUS TALKED TO SOLDIERS, TOO

So that clears away for me the underbrush surrounding our question.

At the beginning it should certainly be realized that Christ did not have this problem to face. I do note, however, that he talked to soldiers in about the same way that he talked to anyone else.

I cannot see in this question any different problem than that presented to every Christian who has to live in our world, except perhaps in degree. When I practice law or build houses or engage in politics, I have to reconcile the ideal of perfection in the Gospels with a world that seems to deny the ideal, that "lieth in wickedness." Every so often laymen have to make choices, not between right and wrong, white and black, but between two grays without a white anywhere near.

If Christianity cannot help them in that dilemma, if they are cast into hellfire or at least into outer darkness because they do make a conscientious choice of the best available course, though they know it carries some evil with it, then you won't have much church left. But that is not my understanding of Christianity at all. The Master of Balliol expressed my views: "It has been the faith of Christians at all times that if they, however stumblingly, aim at carrying out this teaching of Jesus, then their faces will be set towards where the real forward fight is going on, and that, whatever failures they may have to acknowledge, they will have God with them in the midst of the battle to direct and restore."

If you believe, as I do, that God suffers in our failures, then you cannot be happy in any compromise, especially when you realize the danger of a gradual loss of sensitiveness to evil. But to achieve some progress in the end a man may have to choose a course, the very highest he knows, though it carries some effects along with it that he just does not like.

A CHOICE OF GRAYS

Suppose as a member of Congress a person must get the vote of an Italian in order to put through an important piece of social legislation. Italy invades Greece. Shall he satisfy his conscience by a public expression of his condemnation of that act, and lose his measure? Then suppose he has to act on legislation to aid Greece with war supplies. He has to decide which is the more important, from a Christian point of view if he is a Christian—the legislation that needs the Italian vote, or the performance of a duty to speak the truth in condemnation of Italy, or the aid to Greece.

That is what I meant when I said my answer must be in a political frame of reference. For a person to speak out his opinion on an issue to which he is not primarily related and destroy the chance of his primary measure, is a kind of glorified selfishness. The insistence upon an individual standard in the face of the requirements of community responsibility may be just that, and some pacifists are happy because they voluntarily wear that kind of hair shirt. There is a place for martyrdom, as every Christian knows, but some martyrdom is a shirking of responsibility. Between his primary measure and aid to Greece, the Christian must choose, and either choice carries a defeat for the present of some Christian aims.

How does this political frame of reference affect our question?

THE LEADER'S DILEMMA

I begin with the conviction that there is no higher profession than that of political leadership. Oliver put it this way, "Politics is the noblest career that any man can choose." Said Montaigne, certainly no great idealist, "I am of opinion that the most honorable calling is to serve the Public and to be useful to the Many."

A real statesman is always inspired by love of country; with the greatest, patriotism is a passion that overrides every other emotion. It reflects the dynamic of every nation—a strong and permanent love of the soil and the people. It may be like the instinct of the hive, sagacious, undeliberate and fierce. It can be perverted, mere sentiment, or revenge and vindictiveness. But, in the greatest, this love of country, of the soil, the streets, the life and happiness of the people, is not far from Christian. Think of Christ as he looked on Jerusalem and wept. It takes no great imagination to think of Churchill looking on London in the same spirit.

A politician has an instinct for power. Out of power, he can do nothing, not even for those measures for which Christians are lobbying. His first and most imperious duty is to get power and keep it. Power is a very grim thing which mountebanks can rarely hold and handle. A party leader exists to impose broad views upon the narrow, said Morley, but he may not run too far in front of his electorate.

If his policy is nonresistance to aggression, can he stay in power? And if he can, as perhaps he might in Denmark, what happens to his country? A pacifist cannot ignore those questions and be a good Christian. If he can face them intelligently and sincerely, and remain a pacifist, then I say, more power to him. But refusing to think through this terrible dilemma is no adequate basis for martyrdom.

TWO KINDS OF ISOLATIONISM

What policy can a Christian statesman follow when war threatens his country? He knows as well as the ten of us that wars are beastly and often futile; but he knows, too, that on occasion a victory for the wrong side has put civilization back for decades, even centuries. He must be guided solely by the long-term interest of his own people. That is not a shortsighted selfishness or an attempt at an impossible isolationism. England's policies in Manchuria and Ethiopia failed to meet that requirement and were produced by a combination of a widespread, irresponsible pacifism among the people and a shortsighted national selfishness at the head of the government.

Our American attitude in 1920 was subject to the same criticism. The selfish isolationism of petty ward heelers found its reflection in the Senate and later in the White House, and was the beginning of the cynicism and disillusionment that led straight to Hitler and this war. I complain here, not because we and England were not idealists in 1920 and 1931 and 1935, though I don't like that, but because we were not intelligently selfish enough to see our real long-term interests. I say, "America first!" But it can't be first or even safe except by intelligent altruism. It certainly can't be first or safe by co-operating with tyranny abroad. "You can't co-operate with destruction of freedom abroad, without threatening destruction of freedom at home," said Burke. Complete pacifism at home in our situation, which almost certainly would mean the end of British resistance, is exactly that. Pacifists who face that place themselves in exactly the same dilemma as the rest of us. If they choose the ideal for them, it carries evil with it, and they, like the rest of us, must reconcile that evil with the gospel of perfection. Their solution, too, is a choice of grays with a lot of black in them.

WHEN THE OTHER CHOICES ARE WORSE

The choice of a Christian statesman must be deliberate, intelligent, unprejudiced. He must judge of the possible futility and the certain bestiality of war, but he must not shudder and close his eyes to the fact that all other alternatives may be worse. He must have the kind of prejudice against war that kept Cleveland out of Cuba, and guard against the kind of weakness that led us into Cuba later. But force he must certainly use as a tool where nothing else will do the work. The welfare of his people in the years and centuries to come is the only guide he can follow. Again that can be a Christian ideal, at least for the greatest.

The Christian statesman can have a conviction in the ultimate accomplishment of the Kingdom of God even through the storm and travail of this day and generation. He can admit that his own view of that Kingdom may not be God's, and yet work forward according to his best lights. "In the present . . . war it is quite possible that God's purpose is something different from the purpose of either party, and yet the human instrumentalities, working just as they do, are of the best adaptation to effect his purpose." But that view did not prevent Lincoln from forming his policy in the light of the needs of all his people as he saw them, and accepting God's judgment as true and righteous altogether. Said

Churchill, "We shall draw from the heart of suffering itself the means of inspiration and survival."

But the true statesman must accept for his nation the moral responsibility that goes with its long-term interests. We are today one of the three great powers of the world, and the world is a lawless frontier. The bad men of the old frontier were finally routed by the responsible citizens. Those citizens could have "holed up" and built a local defense apparently sufficient for their own protection. Some citizens did just that. But banditry in the community made life unsafe even for them, and the intelligent ones assumed the moral responsibility for the clean-up. They were not "Meddlesome Matties," though the bandits doubtless called them that.

It is quite true that we cannot force on other nations our ideas of what their internal organization should be. But we can certainly prevent that banditry from spreading outside their borders and affecting the peace of the world. The responsibility of a world power for the just organization of world affairs is on us whether we like it or not. There could be no greater and more challenging task. It is a slow, difficult, dangerous one, and to its accomplishment I cannot see that the extreme pacifist point of view contributes anything much. I respect the true pacifist for his single-minded sincerity, and I want him around as a mirror of the ideal of perfection. But I am glad there are not too many of him.

CHAPTER NINE

You're in the Army Now [1]

$\mathcal{Y}$OU BOYS ARE IN THE ARMY NOW—OR practically there. The first thing to do is to learn the ropes with your eyes and ears open and your mouth shut. Relax and be patient and it's surprising how many of your questions are answered sooner than you expect.

You will meet all kinds of people, more kinds even than you find in a boys' school. Don't be disturbed by the way they show off because they are as nervous as you are. Look for things to like in them:

Some of you will not pass the physical. Don't be disturbed by that. There are plenty of chances to serve your country, perhaps even better ones, in the army of civilians.

In either case you are going into the middle of the most interesting problem in life—the problem of how a great mass of people get things done which they all want. It looks different in the Army from what it is in a great city, or a nation of 135,000,000 people, but it isn't. It is all part of what F. S. Oliver called the "endless adventure of governing men." But Oliver was a cynical old dry-goods merchant who was a little discouraged with the basic problem of life and democracy: how to get people to do for themselves.

ARMY BUREAUCRATS

In that process of Running an Army or running a government, you have to have bureaucrats. In fact you have to have them in a business, even a drug store or a grocery store. It is the lack of small competent bureaucrats working in them that explains why so many grocery stores fold up every year. The problem is to find

[1] Talk to Graduation Class, Taft School, Watertown, Conn., Feb. 5, 1944.

good bureaucrats instead of bum ones. You have to have a certain amount of red tape and organization as soon as you deal with people in large numbers. What you need is bureaucrats who make the machinery work. Top sergeants and regimental adjutants and executive officers are more necessary than military geniuses.

ARMY CONFERENCE TECHNIQUE

You will move up in the Army and maybe in the Navy. Remember what Cromwell said: You never go so far as when you don't know where you are going. And as you move up, just as when you return to civilian life and move up, you have to learn how to get people to do things. You have to like them and understand them, but above all you must know that even the ones you like the least usually have something to contribute to your common objectives. Start a powwow around a plan of action and let the group feel they are part of it, and you will find yourself changing the plan bit by bit until the top man decides on the new plan and comes out with something different, and better, than what anyone started with. Only an arbitrary ass refuses to follow the conference method.

That is the only way you can get things done in civilian life. In the Army in the end you obey orders, but at home, unless you bring people along with you, you lose out alone.

STAY WITH A LOUSY ASSIGNMENT

You'll learn the ordinary lessons in the Army, but two will be tough. The first bad one is to stay with a lousy assignment. Do what you can to get a better one, but stay with the one you have. Cromwell's crack about never knowing how far you go, came out of Army life.

LEARN TO FACE DEATH

The toughest lesson of all is to face death. A good many people, especially in these days of soft living, never learn that one. Think it out for yourself and find the chaplain or friend who can help you. Think of the lovely child that died too soon, but holds a sweetness and inspiration for those who knew her that perhaps she never would have achieved by living longer. William Allen White died the other day full of years and I suspect happy in the love of all of us who knew him, but especially happy because his son, Bill, who had wandered the world, had come back home to carry on the *Emporia Gazette*.

And think over this one. Robert Sherrod of *Time* on the beach at Tarawa looked at a Marine horribly dead and said, "What an awful way to die!" And a big Marine sergeant beside him answered, "I don't know a better way."

We're all scared, but we all have to face it. Justice Holmes quoted this old Latin saying, "Death plucks my ear and says, 'Live, for I am coming.'"

THINGS TO LIVE FOR

And what there is to live for! There never was such a day for men, a day of promise or disaster, and all in our hands. We need every kind of useful job. These things that need to be done, can be done if the men are there at the right moment. I can give you samples again and again just from three brief years in Washington— or from twenty years in Cincinnati for that matter—where things were done and results accomplished because a man or a woman was there: otherwise they would not have happened. Sometimes it was the person's regular job; sometimes they were the extra-curricular jobs. Don't let yourself turn into the kind of person that people quit asking. I know a man, well off, that nobody likes to ask for money. I know a man, pleasant, affable, competent, that nobody ever asks to do a job any more, for he never gets them done. I know a lot who always say, "No." Don't let yourself slide into those classes of people. Help get the extra jobs done, and make your own job something that helps to make a new world.

And don't be a cynic. Look at things as they are, but hold onto the promise, *Behold I make all things new*. It has been fashionable to feel that this idealism and church stuff is all right in its way, but you don't have to have it. These other religions abroad are all right and we have no business to send these missionaries over to make them all dissatisfied and cause trouble.

A WORLD OUR NATION CAN LIVE IN

What do you think it is that revolts us with the Japanese atrocities? Our own ancestors used to treat prisoners that way. What has changed this world of ours? There is just one answer to that: Christianity. And it is organized, intelligent Christianity, not people who visit church on Easter, or only at funerals, and figure that after all service and living decently is all you need. Why are the Japs the way they are? For the same reason that headhunters in the Solomons were the way they were. But Christian people from Australia and other places gave their lives there on the equator to turn them into this kind of friendly savages that do tremendous work for our war and rescue our aviators behind the Jap lines and risk their own lives.

No, you can't pass up Shintoism and emperor-worship and military dictatorship with a tolerant wave of the hand. We did that and we got war and atrocities.

That leaves us a tremendous job after this war. We not only have to go on building a nation we can live in at home, but a world our nation can live in. That means facing the problem of Japan and Germany. You couldn't destroy 100,000,000 people if you wanted to. You can't lock them up in a watertight compartment. Sentimentality is just as bad. I don't know the answer, but I know that an intelligent Christian civilization can find it.

You have had a foundation here for intelligent living and for Christian living. Don't be a parasite on this foundation given you by all that have gone before. You have the sword of intelligence and principle. Remember the will of Mr. Valiant-for-Truth. "My sword I leave to him that shall come after me, and my courage and skill to him that can get it."

CHAPTER TEN

The Spiritual Foundations of International Economic Affairs [1]

$\mathcal{F}$OR SPIRITUAL FOUNDATIONS WE LOOK TO religion and its organized expression, the church. The nations in the war for seven or five years are terribly tired, and even in this country military personnel and civilians feel the strain. We are winning the war; but now and after it is won we shall need not only a solidity of foundation but the lift into the clear fresh air of the lofty cathedral spire. That need is an ache inside of us all, of which we may or may not be conscious. The question for a group like this is whether the church is giving that base and that aspiration.

THE ANSWERS FALL SHORT

The church has given, among others, three answers to this problem of war and evil. The first is the answer of the extreme Augustinian, that evil is inevitable in a world like this, and we can only look for relief to the world to come, where the select, saved by grace, achieve blessedness. That does not cheer many of us, though it may be natural enough in a destroyed and suffering Europe.

A second answer is pacifism. No one responsible for the decisions of government, even the small ones, can take that course. It is a rejection of responsibility.

A third and more frequent answer from the church is an attack upon the citadel of big business, the dollar imperialism and the capitalism of evil motives which is said to drive the world into war by fighting for narrowing markets and depleted natural resources.

[1] Talk before the Denver Council of Churches, November 16, 1944. Published in the *Iliff Review*, Winter, 1945.

None of these answers meets the challenge to the church today, and to some degree they suggest in themselves the church's short-coming in this crisis. It is true that the churches have given deep thought to the problems of international organization, and in the "Six Pillars of Peace" have set forth a noble and intelligent statement of objectives. But it is far, far away from both the actual decisions of high policy made in this increasingly critical period of the war, and the daily decisions of the operating administrators of government or of business, which, piled up, come pretty close to making high policy without any decision from on high.

"HAVE–NOT" THEORY DISTORTS FACTS

The extreme emphasis on the economic causes of war seems to me a clear distortion of the facts. It is just as much a distortion as the similar answer of Karl Marx and Engels in the "Communist Manifesto" of 1848. It is not only deeply materialistic, but it is anti-Christian. It makes of capitalism or business or economics a scapegoat, and attributes to capitalists and businessmen motives that are quite unbelievable.

It just doesn't stand up under investigation any more than the materialist interpretation of history stands up. If you take the wars from 1815 to 1914 or even to 1944, only relatively minor conflicts have been due to trade. Never once in their colonial expansion into Africa and their economic penetration of China, did Britain, France, Germany, Russia, or Italy come in conflict. Neither trade nor imperialism really explains the important wars in that period— the Crimean War, the Civil War, the Franco-Prussian War, World War I, or this conflict. The *have* and *have-not* theory was always German propaganda. Sweden was just as much a *have-not* nation as Germany. Politicians of the great powers follow their own judgment, not the profit-line of armament manufacturers.

TAKING IT OUT ON THE OTHER FELLOW

The causes of war lie deep in the human spirit. The most interesting analysis I have seen of the causes of war is in a symposium published six years ago by a group of young British socialists.

They held that war must be regarded as one species of a larger genus, the genus of fighting, a rather universal form of human behavior. So they studied fighting in its simplest forms, among apes and children.

There were three main causes, apparently: (1) fighting over the exclusive right to possession of objects or to the possession of interest and affection, (2) fighting a stranger or outsider because he is an intruder, and (3) fighting or attacking a person or thing because of frustration in one's own activities—"taking it out" on somebody because one is in a bad temper. Being in a bad temper is usually because you are frustrated.

These young Britishers concluded that the primary cause of this fighting or aggression was the same in adult life as among children or apes, plus the factor that people in groups can exhibit a ruthlessness that few individuals would reach in personal contacts. In fact, aggression on a group scale becomes equally simple and direct as a child's fight over possession of a toy. But beyond that, the people of a nation or the dominant groups in it because they don't get what they want or have been persuaded to want may become so frustrated—with such an internal conflict and such hatred of the scapegoat (which their leaders have developed for them at home or abroad) that war is the only outlet, civil war or foreign war.

ANTI-SOCIAL MINORITIES

This analysis has two results. One is pessimism, because it makes it look as if peace were impossible. But that result is only apparent, for all nations, even the warlike, have devoted much more of their energy on a quantitative basis to co-operation and peaceful pursuits than to war. And many nations for centuries have kept peace within their own borders. Peaceful co-operation is the norm, not fighting. How can the predominant impulse to peace be strengthened? That is our problem.

The other result of this analysis is to throw doubt on this tendency to blame capitalism or economic causes solely for war. Such a conclusion by a group of socialists is certainly news.

Their final conclusion is that the fundamental aggressiveness of humans will cause wars unless humans are changed or their aggressiveness restrained. That makes sense. It represents the way we keep the peace at home, while even abroad the great preponderance of human impulses and inclinations and practices is on the side of peaceful co-operation. It is anti-social minorities that cause war, and we are setting out now to restrain them. And this analysis gives the church its two jobs, first trying to eliminate the causes of frustration, bad temper and repression in individual lives, especially in bringing up children; and second, supporting the moral administration of force to restrain aggression while working to eliminate the real causes of national frustration. That is what the Dumbarton Oaks Charter seeks to accomplish; it deserves the hearty support of the churches.

TALK IS POLITICS

A distinguished friend of mine complained bitterly last May that this was going to be a peace of oil, of gold, of shipping, of factual situations, without moral purpose, a peace of dicker and trade, instead of a peace of words—revolutionary words like freedom and democracy.

That conclusion is equally unsound. Stanley King, president of Amherst, wrote some ten years ago that the alternative to war is negotiation, the force of words against the force of arms; and that the way of adjustment, the settlement by talk, is politics, in which the negotiator is the politician. I suppose my friend was sick of politicians. He wanted an upset of the things he didn't like as they were, and quite rightly, I suppose, didn't think a negotiating politician would upset anything.

Perhaps so, but as President King also pointed out, politicians are the salvage men of government who come in after the crisis or revolution and construct. Hamilton, Adams, Madison and Jefferson were politicians, and that meant negotiators and traders, dealers in factual situations.

FACTUAL PEACE

So this is a peace of transportation and trade and finance and ships and land and oil. We shan't have security by way of spiritual foundations without jobs, as the candidates call them, or dignity of labor, as the church describes it. Neither shall we have the aspiration and ambition and risk-taking and progress without the framework of peaceful co-operation in these factual situations around the world.

I want to tell you a little of the scope of the economic problems we face. Every nation in the war except ourselves and Russia faces the problem of paying, with nonexistent or reduced exports, for the essentials of life which they must import. To achieve anything like that, they must finance themselves somehow until they reach the balance of payments. Perhaps we are not directly concerned, selfishly speaking, with some of the devastated areas, but without a restored Great Britain we cannot have a world in which we can be secure. This nation should not and will not accept the controls that go with attempted self-sufficiency. Our resources are not complete within our borders anyway, as we found in this war, and we can't live without the rest of the world.

RESTORING THE ENEMY TO SOCIETY

We have to find how to live with the enemy after we defeat him. We propose to see that he doesn't make war again, but we can't keep him either in an ordianry prison, or in an insane asylum indefinitely, or kill him off. So we have to find how to live with him in the years to come, restricting him in appropriate ways until he shows he can join human society again.

We have some tough problems with distribution and surpluses of commodities—oil, metals, foods, for instance—and the effect of temporary or permanent surpluses on employment.

We have to face the problem of artificial shortages, and government or private monopolies of important commodities or services. Fortunately, the wide difference of background and opinion between England and the United States on this subject is being rapidly narrowed. We may well hope for a united front against the bad practices of cartels.

Transportation and communications is one of our most important problems, in ships, airplanes and radio systems, especially. These will emphasize the difficulties of dependent and backward areas, of colonies and self-government, brought closer and closer in touch with industrial progress and new ideas of all kinds.

A GOOD START AT DUMBARTON OAKS

The Dumbarton Oaks Charter gives a splendid start in the proposed Economic and Social Council. The Assembly of the League was a body essentially political, as it had to be, and by that very fact was often incompetent to deal with economic and social problems. What is now proposed is an over-all international group elected for its qualifications in that specific field, to serve as a forum for the major questions coming up in these various categories of international economic operation.

The members of this Council, like the officers in the economic office of the State Department, will still have to be politicians in the broad sense, that is, negotiators, adjustors, constructors of the means for political co-operation in trade and business and development.

POLITICOS BLOCK SPIRITUAL WORK

The Council members and its United States representatives will be subject to all the alleged disabilities of politicians that make it so difficult for the church to provide a spiritual foundation for international economic order. We representatives of the United States in foreign economic policy can't go straight at our goal usually, for we have to think of the domestic political repercussions—the repercussions in the country we are dealing with, and the effects in third countries. So we move slowly and by the discussion method, which takes endless meetings.

THE CHRISTIAN BLOCKS AT POLITICS

The churches, in particular the Protestant evangelical churches, to one of which I belong myself, have a lot to learn about that political process. By and large the Protestant churches are without affirmative influence in politics—although their negative influence is often considerable—because they have little advice for the responsible official, who is faced with a choice, not between black and white, evil and good, but between grays only. After I said something like this a month ago to a church group, I received a letter from a minister in the audience which read as follows:

> Please don't ask us evangelical churches to compromise on principle. Isn't there too much compromise in the world? . . . If you compromise—then how far? Suppose that Athanasius, Luther, Bunyan, the Pilgrim Fathers, Wesley, suppose these all had compromised?

I WORK IN THE STATE DEPARTMENT

Let me be clear about this. There are two kinds of problems here, pretty well mixed up. Suppose I favor a particular foreign policy which I believe with all my heart is right. But to get it I have to carry it through Congress where it has the opposition of a particular group, the farm group, the manufacturing interests, or labor, for example. But by modification of that policy—I don't like it, but I hope to get rid of it at some future time—I can pick up the necessary votes to get my policy approved. Am I to say that I must have the perfect whole at once, or do I accept the compromise, make the deal? What does my friend say? I can't even take much time to consult about it; I have to take it or leave it. A three-quarter, a half loaf, or none! But the compromise may be such that it sets back the ultimate objective—or does it? Then you have to exercise real judgment. Does the church help the responsible official who has that kind of choice?

LUTHER CHOSE ONE OF TWO GRAYS

But sometimes you have a choice between two evils and no other choice at all. What are we to say when we are attacked at Pearl Harbor? Or rather, what is the President and what is Congress to say? The choice is between a yielding of all we hold dear, and war with its death and destruction. Someone may say the choice was

made earlier and some may claim that we failed to give Japan economic and political opportunity. I don't think the argument is sound, but the earlier choices were equally difficult. For political leaders the choices are usually between grays, not between blacks and whites. Luther had such a choice between the Peasants of the Revolt, and the Princes. Politically his choice in the end was wrong.

The important element is for the responsible official to have a clear vision of his goal, a humble recognition of how far short he falls, but a determination to keep up the fight. Does my friend think he helps anyone by shuddering every time a person says, "compromise"? The fact is that the genius of Anglo-Saxon democratic ideals, which spring so much from the religion of the independent churches like the Baptists and Quakers, is in the acceptance of progress by compromise.

GOD'S WORK

At the same time that I urge on the church an understanding of politicians and of compromise as a basic element in democracy, I suggest also the deepest need of the day, which is supplied basically from religious faith—the conviction that man can help achieve the purposes of God through the years. It may take generations to teach millions of families to bring up children without the repressions and frustrations that cause group aggressions, but the nations can get from religion the conviction that these problems can be solved.

When hostilities stop, there can be a terrible letdown. We cannot let it happen. We must give to our operations in preparation for the next events the sense of urgency and conviction of success that will mean indeed a world of peaceful co-operation with spiritual foundations.

CHAPTER ELEVEN

The People in the Pews[1]

$\mathcal{I}$ HAVE ALREADY EXPRESSED MY PROFOUND sense of this honor,[2] and my feeling that it represents a recognition, perhaps overdue, of the fact that the people in the pews make the Church of Christ.

Again and again we hear it stated that this day of wrath calls for a spiritual revival in which that church and its teaching is the only fundamental recourse.

What is it that the church is supposed to supply to harassed man and mankind?

In attempting to analyze somewhat the problems of our modern world that call for the exercise of the Christian conscience and the expansion of Christian co-operation, it seemed to me that all of those problems had a common characteristic. They can each of them so easily come to look like a living but soulless giant, stupidly, selfishly, senselessly, dangerously blocking the pathway of us sons of light, until there seems no possible way of progress, but only retrogression into the Slough of Despond.

THE CIVIC BLOCK

For instance, I visited a city a few months ago not far from my home town, to speak, for a good government group. They had the support of most of the good people among the business and professional interests. At the last moment the political organizations, both of them, started a vigorous attack, scared some forty witnesses nominated for some of the bad precincts into withdrawing after

[1] Talk before the Federal Council of Churches, Seattle, Wash., Dec. 6, 1946.
[2] The Council in Biennial meeting broke with custom and elected me—a layman—their President.

there was no legal way to replace them, and the election was lost by only two votes or so to a precinct.

Such a defeat shakes the faith of many who stuck through the fight; and for a renewal of the fight you have to start all over, probably worse off than if you had never tried. The "juggernaut of soulless men" in this case—uninterested in good government and perhaps positively interested in bad government—rolls on. What is a Christian to do? Especially when he sees under the fringes of the political cloak, tie-ups with professional gambling and organized vice?

THE LABOR BLOCK

Or take labor strife. If you are closer to labor, you will think of that employer group which seems to be utterly ignorant of how a workman really thinks and doesn't set up a good program to find out; which insists a labor union never helped a workingman anyway, but exists only to promote the interests of the labor boss; and which thinks of nothing but that dream about the return of the good old days when a man could either keep the unions out of the plant or manage the tame little ones that he kept in his pockets. The effort to raise the question even for discussion, meets a complete block in otherwise human beings, and Christian convictions become irrelevant.

These feelings feed on themselves and on opposition. One need hardly be surprised to hear such utter nonsense spouted on the other side as the recent charge by a prominent labor leader of a "widespread and sinister conspiracy of organized monopoly employers to depress wages, establish speedups to pyramid profits, and torpedo living standards of all the people."

THE BLOCK TO PEACE

We face a Russia to whose people a party-line version of what goes on in the world outside is fed in huge and continuing doses, a version which most unfortunately and dangerously is apparently believed also by their leaders. Those leaders are conditioned in a philosophy which rejects as silly our Christian emphasis on the supreme importance of the individual soul, and which looks with contempt on our scruples about the means to achieve a doctrinaire purpose. Before that huge mass, insensitive to what we hold dear and apparently insensitive to the entire outside world—unreachable even if the iron curtain were removed—what does one do? The atomic bomb, serious as it is, does not change the fundamental and profoundly difficult problem of how to live with international neighbors with whom we disagree violently. The bomb only makes the problem more dramatic.

THE SECTARIAN BLOCK

The controversy over organic union between different communions may seem to some a little puny alongside these and other national and international problems. But even in such discussions of a religious character one gets the feeling often that the people on the other side are a solid unmoving deaf giant which our weak capacities can never defeat except by main force. We cannot get our words through their defenses to their intelligence—we are tempted by the devil to say "if any." Our feeling about some of our Roman Catholic brethren can easily reach the same hopeless defeatism if we permit it.

What is it that our Christian church is supposed to be able to offer us laymen, caught in that kind of nightmare? I speak quite frankly, as, you remember, Justice Brewer did once fifty years ago—from the pew to the pulpit. I am a little afraid that perhaps you haven't developed, or at least made available, what we need. Many of you don't even study our problems from that angle.

TRADITIONAL CURES

We are offered traditionally an evangelical campaign to convert our domestic heathen friends and bring them into the church. Perhaps that is part of the answer. Certainly I favor it. A very acute analysis made a few years ago of our modern civilization's tendency to war, centered its attack on the individual and group tendency to grab, to kill the outlander, and to explode in a vicarious reaction from piled-up personal and national frustrations. Only a forthright effort to achieve individualized sharing of our best traditions, including our religious faith, can overcome those individual tendencies that show up from early childhood.

Nevertheless, as a solution for Ku-Kluxery or a Yugoslav "incident," that method is less than satisfactory to a responsible leader or a responsible observer.

Verbal fireworks, usually intemperate, always without responsibility, and based primarily on the technique which in its uncivilized form blackens the female ancestry of your opponent, has certain unfortunately soothing effects on the ego. The Christian versions of this technique are not uncommon. We damn Russia, or damn those who damn Russia, for example. Delivered under the aegis of liberalism, they are to me singularly unattractive and un-Christian.

Sometimes fine people who discover and struggle with these giants of obstruction for the first time in hitherto secluded lives, come up with a decision in favor of war to the death. This is the technique that kills the giant dead because you can't persuade him, or beats the baby till he sneezes.

THE RELEVANCE OF REVIVALISM

What do we laymen look for from the Christian Church? If Christian beliefs are really important, they ought to help us face and resolve this mess at home and abroad.

The evangelicals of the revival a hundred and more years ago emphasized the personal depravity of each man and the absence of any "particle of inherent righteousness" in the miserable sinner. Only conversion of a kind that is fixed at an identifiable moment, the vicarious atonement of Jesus, and the justification that comes completely dissociated from anything else the sinner does, could save any of us in those days. They had little appreciation of liturgical beauty. Belief in the verbal inspiration of the Bible made a pretty complete whole, all of which can still be found today in the new churches at which we are accustomed to look a little down our noses. The membership of the Church of God or of the Nazarene certainly shows the effectiveness of the old-time religion, even though we Episcopal evangelicals may be convinced it is not a solution, at least in those terms, to our modern problem. It represented a great advance in its day over the disgraceful state of the churches in the days before the Wesleyan revival.

But the other doctrines of the early nineteenth-century evangelicals are as fresh as they were one hundred and fifty years ago. They looked to Jesus, the author and finisher of our faith, and to the Scriptures for everything necessary to the health of their souls. They believed in baptism and the Lord's Supper, and these sacraments were neither sacerdotal nor sacrificial, but deeply emotional and recreating.

THE ROYAL PRIESTHOOD

Our predecessors referred to the royal priesthood of the whole body of Christians, which means that each person has a direct approach to God, through Jesus, if need be, as the only mediator, without the necessity of priest intervening. He is a minister in his sphere of the Grace of God.

Now, I am a politician with some labor and foreign affairs experience. The part of those evangelical beliefs which I find most important to me in this perplexing world is, you may be surprised to know, the priesthood of all believers, that royal priesthood of all faithful people. For that very basic element in the Protestant Reformation and a part of the reform of the Church of England is clearly the basis, too, for the development of political democracy as we Americans understand it. Political democracy has proven itself the handmaiden of peaceful living among nations, even the modern nation-states. Not that we democracies avoid all responsibility for this last Thirty Years' War, but it is a bit hard, you will agree, to conceive of war between us and England, us and France, us and Sweden. The nearest approach to a world government yet is the British Commonwealth of Nations.

Let me tell you a little about how this doctrine of the priesthood of all believers produced democracy in the days when the Reformation was not history but a living, dynamic reality.

In 1647 Cromwell had defeated the King, and the Episcopalians, with Laud, were completely out of power. The New Model Army was all Puritan, but was made up of three completely different groups: the Presbyterians, who wanted a state church with no toleration for anybody else; the Independents, of whom Cromwell and Ireton were the leaders, the moderates in the middle of the road; and the left-wingers, of whom at this stage the Levelers who stood for complete liberty of conscience, were the most important. The Independents were the Congregationalists; Levelers, the successors to the Anabaptists and brothers in spirit to the Baptists and Quakers.

The question before them in 1647 was what should be the form of the new government, which strove to bind the King and prevent absolutism—political or, as the Levelers insisted, religious.

The representatives of the left-wing Levelers, company by company, were appropriately enough known as Agitators. Their proposals were the subject of a debate in the Council of the Army on October 27 and 29, 1647, at Putney. We know what they said because it was taken down in shorthand by Clarke, the Secretary of the Army.

Nearly the entire debate centered on Proposition No. 1. It read as follows:

I. That the people of England, being at this day very unequally distributed by counties, cities, and boroughs, for the election of their deputies in Parliament, ought to be more indifferently proportioned, according to the number of inhabitants.

Ireton interrupted at once. "The meaning is that every man that is an inhabitant is to be equally considered, and to have an equal voice in the election of those representatives; and if that be the meaning, then I have something to say against it."

Then Colonel Rainborough spoke the new words. "For really I think that the poorest he, that is in England, hath a life to live, as the greatest he; and, therefore, truly, sir, I think it's clear that every man that is to live under a government ought first by his own consent to put himself under that government."

Ireton almost sputtered as he replied: "No man hath a right to an interest or a share in the disposing of the affairs of the Kingdom, and in determining or choosing those that shall determine what laws, we shall be ruled by here—no person hath a right to this, that hath not a permanent fixed interest in this kingdom . . . that is, the persons in whom all land lies, and those in corporations[1] in whom all trading lies. . . . If you admit any man that hath a breath and being, why may not these men vote against all property?"

"Every man born in England," Rainborough answered, "cannot, ought not, Neither by the law of God nor the law of nature, to be exempted from the choice of those who are to make laws for him to live under, and for him, for ought I know, to lose his life under. What hath the soldiers fought for all this while?"

Cromwell in this debate was on Ireton's side, yet there was in him far more understanding of this almost mystical faith in the ordinary man. Cromwell was also the practical man. The Levelers meant to require unanimity, or individual revolution. There Cromwell drew the practical line, which in fact became the democratic decision of the majority. "When anything is spoken as from God, I think the rule is, let the rest judge. . . . I do not judge conclusively, negatively, that it was not of the Lord but I do desire to submit it to all your Judgments whether it was of the Lord or no. Truly we have heard many speaking to us; and I cannot but think that in most that have spoke there hath been something of God laid forth to us; and yet there have been several contradictions in what hath been spoken. But certainly God is not the author of contradic-

---

[1] I.e. cities.

tions . . . I cannot see but that we all speak to the same end, and the mistakes are only in the way."

Rainborough and the Levelers lost out in that argument, but forty years later when John Locke wrote the justification for the Glorious Revolution of 1688 it was Rainborough's doctrine that governments exist by the consent of the governed, that was the basis of the argument.

DEMOCRACY OUT OF THE REFORMATION

From Locke to the French to Jefferson was the way the Declaration of Independence and its spirit of equality came into our American political life. Even then every man, much less woman, could not vote. Only one in twenty-five was eligible to vote for the State Conventions which ratified our Constitution. Not until 1850 did the last American state eliminate the property qualification for voting. Only in this century did the British reach the ideal of the Levelers.

Yet that practice of equality and discussion and decision in the small independent congregations of the seventeenth century is surely the first beginning of our Anglo-Saxon democratic inheritance. And it comes right from the belief that God speaks direct to laymen, the priesthood of all believers.

You and I take for granted the procedure of a committee meeting under Robert's Rules of Order—a chairman, a secretary, minutes, motion, discussion, amendments; vote, and passage or defeat by a majority vote on most issues (or two-thirds or even three-fourths on special matters). But the Russians as a people had never had as late as twenty years ago any experience in that at all. Even now their really democratic experience in our sense is restricted to their co-operatives. There is none in their Soviets, where there is little choice of issues and the "Party" dominates, from the top.

COMMITTEE ACTION AND THE ABSOLUTIST

Deeper than the form of Robert's Rules is the experience of a committee discussion of a really tough issue, in which a group of men of good will can come through a long battle perhaps, with a conclusion in which all can substantially agree and which is different from the position at which any one of them started. Or perhaps there still remains a difference of opinion. But it has been limited to the bare bones of the real issue: a majority has decided one way, and the rest loyally accept the conclusion, even though they may at the same time set out to change by persuasion their minority to a majority.

Our democratic problem really begins when you try to apply that technique to a city or state of 200,000 to 12,000,000 or to a nation of 140,000,000. That problem we have yet to solve fully; but it is exactly here that you need the faith of the Christian, which is based on the priesthood of all believers. It is the conviction, which is almost mystical, that somehow, some way, on the issues that are basic, the individual souls who make up the people can come to conclusions which in the long run are indeed such as to work the will of God. It is a conviction that the bogey we conjure up of a destroying mass mind or a merely obstructive dull giant does not in fact exist. We make the venture of faith that this is, or can be made into, a world of individual children of God who want his will to prevail, if you give them a chance to look at and understand the choices.

The enemy of that whole position is the absolutist. When the people refuse to accept the position he advocates, he can believe only that they are wrong. He cannot wait for them to be persuaded, and he is tempted to force them to accept his position. He is often so impressed with the importance of what he believes in, that any evil in the means used to compel acceptance, becomes colored with the virtue of his objective. That was what happened to employers who employed labor spies and provocateurs and brutal guards; and to union leaders who closed their eyes to dynamiting and sabotage. The evil means used on one side produce corresponding reactions. The absolutism of the extreme Zionist and of the extreme Arab nationalist is bound to end in conflict, and can even produce condemnation of its own best leaders when they seek sensible solutions, as witness the recent attacks on Chaim Weizman. The extreme absolutism of the extreme Catholic matches the un-Christian Protestant.

THE ROLE OF THE POLITICIAN

The only person who understands the essential problems of healing labor strife, or Palestinian rows, or United States relations to the Soviets, or Episcopal Presbyterian Union is the politician. His life study is the technique of persuading a large group of people to move in a particular direction.

There are politicians not only in government but in business, in labor, in churches, and in any other human enterprises where one of the essentials of success is persuading people in numbers to do things the way the persuader wants them done.

I have used a word, "politician"; and it has created in your minds, first, amusement, and then all the evil connotations of bribery and corruption, expediency and deception, talk without matter, and compromise of principles. Even those of you, whom, if I knew the Federal Council a little better, I could point out as consummate politicians, are probably thinking I should better have avoided the word. I deny it. I am a politician myself. It is high time that men of religion, both clerical and lay, should face up to their responsibilities in life, and politics is one of those responsibilities.

IS IT CHRISTIAN TO COMPROMISE?

Let me take the last connotation of "politician" suggested above, "compromise of principle."

We follow a Master who laid down a counsel of perfection. Certainly I am not denying that counsel. That ideal of perfect living is in fact the fascinating goal that wins the utter allegiance and lifelong effort of every one of you here tonight. But I deny that the Sermon on the Mount is a code of laws or ethics even for Christians. A code is something which is generally accepted by the entire group which it governs as the way in which they and their fellows will generally and actually live. The Sermon on the

Mount is not that. Some of the statements of the Sermon on the Mount we not only do not live by, but we do not think we can live by them. When a man goes to law with you in a suit which is in effect blackmail, it is your Christian duty to fight him, not to give him twice what he asks. Most of the Sermon on the Mount I will strive to live by—to love my enemies, to bless them that curse me, and the rest. When I fail, I will know that the most important objective of the Sermon on the Mount is that I should, with a humble and contrite heart, know when I have failed, that I am, in that, a despicable sinner, and that I must do better the next time. When I see others failing, and when I see injunctions of the Sermon on the Mount which are today impossible of fulfillment for most, then I need to have the same deep and humble sorrow that we have not yet built a world in which such perfection is possible, and stir my weary associates and my thrice weary self to new plans and efforts.

So I deny that compromise is necessarily evil. Far from that, I assert that compromise is the great invention of the Anglo-Saxons which made democracy possible and that it was a solution arrived at by devoted Christians. Let me recall to you again what Cromwell said: "When anything is spoken as from God, I think the rule is, Let the rest Judge."

Let me remind you also of Gamaliel when Peter came before the Sanhedrin, "If this enterprise springs from men, it will collapse; whereas, if it really springs from God, you will be unable to put them down. You may even find yourselves fighting God."

Granted, there are bad compromises. Poor politicians make really bad compromises of principle and excuse themselves on the unsound ground of practical necessity. It is the great politician who knows how to advance by intelligent compromises. Lord Reading once said that he never compromised with his principles, but only with the tempo of achieving them.

ABSOLUTISM AND WAR

What happens where sound and intelligent compromise is rejected by the absolutist? What happens is war! Before 1688, when an English politician lost an election he lost his head. Think of Raleigh, More, and Charles himself. They died on the block when they guessed wrong. Though Cromwell executed the King and was in many ways the absolutist himself, though the Levelers failed to achieve manhood suffrage and their extremists were absolutists too, yet the result of their coalition was compromise and peace and in the end democracy. It came to that end because they listened to God and listened to God speaking through others.

You of the pulpit recognize the necessity yourselves. It is only the word, compromise, which you shun. You have your own way to describe it. The highest Anglican authority, whom I shall not name, describes it as "some happy way to synthesize your differences."

With some things you cannot compromise, for to compromise sets you farther from your goal of perfection. How do we know what those are? I assure you, politicians need the help of the church there, but they get along nevertheless more successfully without the church than the church gets along without politicians. A counsel of perfection is not much good to us. Our problem is how to produce that little step forward that marches toward the goal we long for.

ALL SORTS AND CONDITIONS OF MEN

The politician has a surprisingly Christian way of understanding of, and sympathy for, all kinds of people. He knows more kinds than even you do. As J. C. Oliver wrote in defense of the politician, he "fights and fraternizes with all sorts and conditions of men. He cannot listen day after day to his opponents [in Congress, for instance] without shaking off much of his original narrowmindedness."

He would never make the statement made by Dr. Urey as quoted in the *New York Times*. A disappointed idealist who has much to learn about the government of men, he said that the United States might have to "declare war ourselves with the frank purpose of conquering the world and ruling it as we desire, and preventing

any other sovereign nation from developing mass weapons of war."
That, gentlemen, is a shocking denial, of a kind which no politician
would believe, far less state, of the divine capacity of human personalities in direct touch with God, to work out solutions.

I hear similar pleas against the old diplomacy and power politics.
Do you like open squabbles like those in Paris, by which a nation
is driven in public to extreme positions from which it cannot with-
draw without loss of face, not merely the "face" of the nation, but
the "face" of the political party in power at home? I could criticize
the political direction of our foreign policy in the last three years
much better than any of you can do, because I know a good deal
about it from the inside. But I say to you that there can be no
direction of foreign policy, as of other fields of government, except
a political direction, because government and foreign relations are
politics. The churches must understand that, must study politics,
and must find a gospel which helps a Christian politician.

Our Anglo-Saxon churches are so ignorant of politics that their
distinguished representatives at the great Oxford Conference in
1937, serving on the Subcommission on Church and State, did not
even know our fundamental political theory derived from John
Locke, and in turn from the Levelers' Christian theory that the
State is no divine and mystical entity, created by God to protect
us in a world of evil, but just a tool created by the community to
perform services for us—a vehicle through which individual
Christians may strive to bring about God's will for men.

GIVE US A MODERN EVANGEL

We laymen need desperately a Christian evangel, expressed in
modern terms, adapted to modern methods. I believe the Federal
Council can do some pioneering in this field, by expanding its research and studies to the importance given study in the Faith and
Order and Life and Work movements, and now in the World
Council; and the study must be in the context of all the best technical knowledge and thought on the world's affairs, not the left
wing only.

Can we devise a political system of conducting our foreign affairs so as to avoid war with Russia and build friendly relations with her and the rest of the world? Certainly we can. It is a deeply technical problem, but it can be illuminated by Christian idealism in the men at the top and down the line.

Can we bring about better labor relations? Certainly, by study of how to deal with men and women in an organization. That is a technique by itself, and a tough one to master, but Christians can make it work at its best.

Can we bring about good government for our cities? Yes, but besides the techniques of politics it takes guts and endurance. It was no accident that three great early leaders of our successful movement in Cincinnati—successful both in accomplishment and duration beyond any other—were, one, a devout Jew, and the other two, strong members of our own Christ Episcopal church.

Can we solve the problem of unity among diverse Christian communions? Yes, by the two great Christian commandments. *Thou shalt love the Lord thy God with all thy strength and mind and heart.* That means loving him where he shines in such liturgies as our Episcopal Book of Common Prayer with its lovely services, and in our Bible in all its fascinating translations of his Word. *Thou shalt love thy neighbor as thyself.* Does not the story of the Good Samaritan teach the Christian ministry of all believers? But to achieve unity we need most of all the true Christian humility that finds God working through other men than ourselves, and listens there too for His consecrated voice.

Bibliography

Gooch, *English Democratic Ideas in the 17th Century*. Cambridge
    University Press.
Lindsay, A. D., *Essentials of Democracy*. Oxford University Press
                Moral Teachings of Jesus. Hodder and Stoughton.
Oliver, J. S., *Politics and Politicians*. MacMillan.
Woodhouse, *Puritanism and Liberty*. Dent.
War and Democracy: essays on the causes and prevention of war by
    E. F. M. Durbin and others. Routledge.

Date Due